Who Came Before

Who Came Before

The Story of Lydia DePiero and Renato Belli

Lynn Belli Fiori

Genealogy House
Amherst, Massachusetts

Published by Genealogy House, a division of White River Press
Amherst, Massachusetts • genealogyhouse.net

ISBN: 978-1-887043-96-0

Book and cover design by Lufkin Graphic Designs
Norwich, Vermont • www.LufkinGraphics.com

All photos from the author's collection unless otherwise attributed.

Library of Congress Cataloging-in-Publication Data

Names: Fiori, Lynn Belli, 1941- author.
Title: Who came before : the story of Lydia Depiero and Renato Belli / Lynn Belli Fiori.
Description: Amherst, Massachusetts : Genealogy House, [2022] | Summary: "A history of the Italian immigrant experience of the author's grandparents and parents, and how her parents built a life together in America. With charts, photos, maps"-- Provided by publisher.
Identifiers: LCCN 2021060207 | ISBN 9781887043960 (hardcover)
Subjects: LCSH: Belli, Renato, 1897-1987. | Belli, Lydia Depiero, 1906-1985. | Belli family. | Italian Americans--New Jersey--Biography. | Italian Americans--New Jersey--Social life and customs. | Italian American families--New Jersey. | New Jersey--Biography.
Classification: LCC F145.I8 F56 2022 | DDC 974.9/004510092 [B]--dc23/eng/20211222
LC record available at https://lccn.loc.gov/2021060207

Contents

Lydia DePiero and Renato Belli on their wedding day,
October 2, 1926.

Prologue

Lydia DePiero and Renato Belli Wed

SATURDAY, OCTOBER 2, 1926 was a sunny, warm, autumn day just perfect for a wedding when Lydia DePiero and Renato Victor Belli were married at Sacred Heart Church on Clifton Avenue, Clifton, N.J. It was a very simple affair. The matron of honor was Lydia's sister Anna DePiero Turrin. The best man was Renato's brother Luigi. There were no bridesmaids or ushers. Angelo DePiero dropped his daughter off at the church but didn't stay to walk her down the aisle. *Mamma* Giuseppina lived only a couple of blocks away but didn't attend. The only attendee was Catherine Marmoci, wife of Romolo, Renato's first cousin. Romolo and Catherine had recently been married. The next year their first child, Norma, would be born on Lydia and Renato's wedding anniversary; and Lydia and Renato's first, Florence, would be born on Catherine and Romolo's anniversary (September 13).

Even at age 20, Lydia aspired to do things right. Her gown was of the latest fashion—a white lace, tea-length skirt with scalloped hem; the bodice with round neckline and short sleeves. With this she wore a Juliette cap with an 8' veil and elbow-length fingerless gloves. She carried a large bouquet of white and red roses. Renato wore a made-to-measure suit, which he wore again forty-seven years later at the marriage of their youngest child.

After the ceremony, the wedding party repaired to Renato's brother John's home for breakfast. The ceremony would have been Mass at which Communion was served. At that time, a Catholic was obligated to fast overnight before receiving Communion, so the bride and groom would have been quite ready for a light meal. From there it was on to Fort Lee, N.J., for a wedding dinner. With no guests at the church, there was no reception. This has always been a puzzlement, but a little research taught me that in 1926 many couples did without a reception. Also, it was the custom for the groom in Italian-American weddings to foot the bill not only for the reception but also for the couple's home and its furnishings. Renato had already built the house at 111 Bergen Avenue and paid for the furnishings, so doing without a reception might have been a cost-cutting measure. Besides, Prohibition was in effect. After the dinner in Fort Lee, Lydia and Renato boarded the night boat for Boston, where they spent the next few days.

A ditty popular in 1926 for choosing your wedding day:

Wednesday is the best day of all but choose
Monday for wealth,
Tuesday for health,
Thursday for crosses,
Friday for losses,
Saturday for no luck at all.

With a marriage that lasted fifty-nine years, Lydia and Renato certainly proved this rhyme false.

Since this important day, much has been written and orally passed on about Renato's family but much less about Lydia's. So, several years ago, I decided to learn more about the DePieros.

Chapter 1

Angelo DePiero

I STARTED AT THE PARISH CHURCH of Santa Maria Maggiore in Cordenons, Italy, birthplace of Lydia and her father. Cordenons is a small town in the region of Friuli-Venezia Giulia in northeast Italy, halfway between Venice and Trieste. At the church I found records of my *Nonno* (Grandfather) Angelo DePiero's family going back to the sixteenth century! So the DePieros were a well-established family there when Angelo Marco was born on April 4, 1866. He was the son of Antonio DePiero del Nut and Teresa Gardonio del Mul. Del Nut and del Mul are nicknames to distinguish one DePiero or Gardonio family from another, just as Codan is used in San Vito to distinguish one Belli family from another.

The use of del Nut goes back as far as Giovanni (Zuanne/ Zanut, pronounced Zanoot in dialect), who was called "Nut." Giovanni was born on March 23, 1607, so he is considered the founder of this DePiero family. Over the years, this information underwent embellishment until it became the story of Angelo's grandfather having had his clothes stolen as he was skinny-dipping and thus returning home "nut (noot)" or nude. As for Teresa Gardonio del Mul, "mul" stands for mulato. For hundreds of years, Cordenons was part of the

Republic of Venice which traded all over the world. Interracial marriages would not have been uncommon. Shakespeare even wrote of one.

At birth, Lydia's father, Angelo, had an older brother Luigi. Over the next fourteen years, three more brothers and four sisters arrived at the rate of one every two years. One sister and one brother died in infancy. Two brothers, Osvaldo and Giuseppe, and three sisters, Rosa, Maria, and Mariana Pasqua, survived. Osvaldo eventually settled in Park Ridge, N.J., and became a farmer raising fruit and vegetables. DePiero's Farm was a landmark in the town until six or seven years ago. It's now a Wegmans supermarket, and the DePiero family has opened DePiero's Farm Stand about a mile from the original spot.

At 20 years of age, Angelo dutifully presented himself to the military authorities in Udine, in order to be enrolled for the draft. According to the record of his physical exam, he was 5'9" tall with curly brown hair and brown eyes. He was rejected for military service due to atrophy of his left arm, which was slightly shorter than the right one. This was probably the result of a birth trauma known as Erb's palsy in which the nerves in the neck are damaged when the head is pushed down and to the side to facilitate passage past the pubic bone. One shoulder is rotated forward, and the affected arm is diminished in length and girth; the muscle of the affected arm will atrophy, and the wrist will be deformed. Depending on the severity of the injury, it can sometimes be corrected with physical therapy or surgery. In 1866, I doubt anything was done. Angelo's disability would have made most kinds of physical labor difficult and would have prevented him from learning a useful trade. It would affect the rest of his life. This handicap was never mentioned when family members spoke of him. However, if one looks closely in photographs, one can detect it. In formal photographs his left hand is positioned firmly on the arm of the chair. In informal ones his hand is in his pocket or resting on his left leg. Also his left eye slightly droops, another symptom of Erb's palsy.

From 1886 to 1891, I found no trace of Angelo. Family legend has it that he spent two years in Argentina, but I can find no trace of him there. However, in speaking with Ed DePiero of Park Ridge (Osvaldo's grandson and my second cousin), I learned that more than one of Angelo's brothers immigrated to Argentina to work in the coal mines before coming to the U.S. I can find no record of Angelo's entry into the U.S. According to the 1900 U.S. Census, he had entered the country in 1891. Ellis Island was not opened until 1892. Until 1890, immigrants entered at Castle Garden in lower Manhattan. From 1890–1892, they entered at a place called the Barge Office. This was a place of complete chaos. So it's possible that when Angelo disembarked, he was overwhelmed by the situation and was unable—or didn't bother—to register.

Many years ago a friend of mine here in New Jersey took a Caribbean cruise. Upon return she told me she had met a woman on the cruise who looked just like me. But she wasn't from Italy. She was from Argentina! Who knows?

CHAPTER 2

Giuseppina Varettoni

N*ONNA* (GRANDMOTHER) Giuseppina Varettoni Carletto (Carletto being the nickname) was born in Borca di Cadore, Italy. Cadore is a small region northwest of Venice nestled in the Dolomite Mountains. Borca is a small town with a population of about 800. It is the first town south of San Vito, Renato Belli's hometown.

I started my research at the Ufficio Anagrafe in the Municipio of Borca. The clerk there, Matteo DeMonte, was eager to help and dug through three or four old registers to find information about Giuseppina. He also gave me the name of Giovanna Varettoni as a local contact who might know more. I returned on another morning to find her. I asked at a florist shop for the address Matteo had given me. There was a customer there who turned out to be Matteo's brother—but neither he nor the florist knew of Giovanna. Then in walked the wife of the mayor. She didn't know of Giovanna either, but offered to take me to the mayor.

Because it's taken for granted that in small town Italy the mayor knows everything about everyone, his wife walked me back to the municipio. On the way I explained that I'm a Belli Codan, first cousin of Guido Belli. Guido happened to be an influential retired businessman in San Vito, so I figured she would know him. She then made a point of telling me she is a Menegus, "an important name in San Vito." The municipio was locked, but Signora "Mayor" whipped out her cell phone and called the mayor to come down and open the doors. He did. And he knew Giovanna. Only everyone calls her Gianna, which was why no one had recognized her name. From Giovanna to Gianna might not seem like a very big leap, but it is if you live in Borca or even in San Vito. These mountain people are set in their ways.

Signora "Mayor" then took me to Gianna's address, but she wasn't home, so I called later and made a date for the next day. It turned out she could add nothing to what I already knew about the family.

Giuseppina Varettoni was born at 11:00 a.m. on January 19, 1874 in the Villanova section of Borca di Cadore, Italy. At the Ufficio Anagrafe in Borca, I learned that her father, Bortolomeo, was a shoemaker. At his birth, August 16, 1829, he had an older brother, Pietro and, later, four more siblings: Giovanni, Maddalena, Baldassare, and Teresa. As adults, Giovanni and Baldassare relocated to Venice where they made cones for ice cream. Baldassare's great-grandaughter, Gianna, is the woman I met in Borca. She is the last surviving cousin of ours there. The name Varettoni comes from the word *veriton*, meaning a person who makes arrow-throwers, a weapon used by hunters until 25,000 years ago when it was supplanted by the bow. Today the word is still used by some.

On August 7, 1871, Bortolomeo (Bortolo) had married Maria Sala. They had two daughters, Giuseppina and her older sister. Maria Sala died of unknown causes on December 24, 1884, and her older daughter died a few years later. Bortolo then married his wife's sister. (Renato's brother Albino Belli also married his wife's sister when his first wife died.)

As a young girl, Giuseppina learned to weave, probably from her mother. In 1887, after digging the soil by hand, she planted some flax seeds. She cultivated the plants, cut and dried the stalks, cleaned the fiber, carded the strands and spun them into linen thread, set up the warp in a loom, and then wove the threads into a sheet. This she hemmed and added her initials in red on the border. This sheet became part of her dowry, and she brought it with her when she came to America. (What a powerful connection this sheet became to our roots in Italy. It is the Holy Grail of the DePieros; a tangible piece of family history. I inherited it from my mother, Lydia, and today, when I hold it, tears come to my eyes. I will pass it on to one of my daughters who will pass it on to her daughter.)

Relations were strained between Giuseppina and her stepmother, and in 1892, at the age of 18, Giuseppina immigrated to America. She arrived at Ellis Island on the SS *La Champagne* on May 30, 1892. Aunt Anna, Lydia's sister, wrote that Giuseppina was going to live in Clifton, N.J. with a family named Perini. There were families of this name in Borca, but I have been unable to find any trace of the one Giuseppina might have lived with in Clifton. Pina, as she was familiarly known, found work as a weaver, the trade she had learned in Italy. She most probably lived in the Botany Village section of Clifton. Botany Woolen Mills were just across the border in Passaic, and Forstmann Woolen Company was also nearby.

I have been unable to trace Angelo once he got off the boat in New York. In 1891, he had no other immediate family here. He had no specific trade, probably because of his handicap, and declared himself a "laborer in a quarry" in the 1900 U.S. Census. However, he must have been in Clifton sometime after 1892 in order to meet Giuseppina. How they met and how their courtship progressed is anybody's guess. The fact is that they were married on July 21, 1895 in the Church of St. Joachim in lower Manhattan. My mother, Lydia, always said they were married in the "Little Church Around the Corner"; Aunt Anna also states this in her "Remembrances." The church in Manhattan with this nickname is an Episcopal church on E. 29th St., just off Fifth Avenue, nowhere near lower Manhattan and has no record of them. So maybe Giuseppina meant "the little church around the corner" . . . without capital letters. The Church of St. Joachim no longer exists. It was torn down many years ago to make way for an apartment building, and its parish merged with that of the Church of St. Joseph nearby.

I found a copy of their marriage license and marriage certificate at the Manhattan Hall of Records. They both give their place of residence as 155 7th St. in Passaic, N.J. This street no longer exists. Could this have been a boarding house? Is it where they met? Would they have remained there after they married? It is curious that they went to New York to be married when there were a couple of churches nearby in Passaic. Were "destination" weddings popular even then?

Angelo and Giuseppina's firstborn, a son, father of Jen DePiero Kimball, was born in June 1896 in Passaic. He was named Attilio, but he was always called John. Was "Attilio" too difficult for non-Italians to understand? In fact, in the 1900 U.S. Census, he is listed as Achiolio. Shortly thereafter, the family moved to Brandywine, Pennsylvania, where Angelo could find work. In October 1897, another son was born. He was named Antonio but was always known as Uncle Jack to us nieces and nephews. Another son, Bortolo, arrived in March 1899, just seventeen months after Antonio. Unfortunately, Bortolo did not survive more than eighteen months.

In Brandywine they rented a home, and Giuseppina took in boarders. Lydia always said it was her mother's dream to run a boarding house. This requires good organizational abilities, which must have been passed on to Lydia and then from Lydia to Florence and me. Among other things I remember is Giuseppina's way of folding and ironing sheets. First you fold the sheet lengthwise with the wrong sides out. Then fold it again with the top quarter of the sheet on top. Then flip the top quarter back. Now the right side of the whole top half of the sheet is contained in the two top folds. This way you can iron the whole top half of the sheet in one operation. The bottom half is never seen so really doesn't need to be ironed. I still iron my sheets this way. I have tried to teach this method to my daughters, but ironing sheets seems to have gone out of fashion.

The 1900 U.S. Census notes that the DePieros had two boarders, a male of 36 years and a female of 59. As previously mentioned, Angelo stated his occupation as "laborer in a quarry."

On September 24, 1900 in Wilmington, Delaware, Angelo DePiero was granted the right of U.S. Citizenship. As his wife, Giuseppina automatically became a citizen also. This gave them the possibility to travel to and from Italy freely. It also gave the right to citizenship to their children born in Italy, namely Mary (b. 1901), Lydia (b. 1906), and Guido (Bill) (b. 1908).

Shortly after being granted citizenship, Angelo and family returned to Cordenons, probably because Angelo was unable to find work in Delaware. This marked the beginning of thirteen years of traveling back and forth with no fixed job or residence. When the family packed up all their belongings and left for Italy, Giuseppina, 26, had just buried a son under age 2; had two sons, ages 5 and 4; and was pregnant with their fourth child. According to Aunt Anna, Angelo and Giuseppina were building a house in Cordenons at that time. When they arrived it was still unfinished. Giuseppina felt the house was not ready for a newborn, so she took the two boys and went to her father's home in Borca di Cadore. Their first daughter, Mary, was born there in February.

When Mary was born, it was law that the father of the infant must register the newborn at the town hall. Since Mary's father was not present, the clerk registered her as illegitimate, and as a surname gave her *Delle Rocchette*, meaning "of the Rocks," a group of local mountains. In 1957 Lydia, who was vacationing nearby in San Vito, went to obtain a copy of Mary's birth certificate and discovered the error. You can bet she insisted on correcting it.

CHAPTER 3

Returning to America . . . and Back to Italy

ON JULY 14, 1901, Angelo is listed on the manifest of the SS *L'Aquitaine* out of Le Havre, France. He gives his place of residence as Wilmington. No other family members are listed, so he might have come looking for work. Besides, Mary would have been only a couple of months old.

On April 14, 1902, Angelo again enters the U.S., this time accompanied by his youngest brother, Giuseppe, who would have been 22 years old. They are listed on the ship's manifest of a French ship, the SS *La Champagne*. No other family members are listed, but they must have been with him. The ship's manifest is a "List of Alien Immigrants for the Commissioner of Immigration." Since Giuseppina and the children were U.S. citizens, perhaps that is why they are not listed.

Aunt Anna writes that they went to live in Passaic, where she was born on February 29, 1904. By 1906, Angelo, Giuseppina and their four children were back in Cordenons, probably, again, because Angelo could not find work. The city of Passaic and a large part of northern New Jersey had suffered a devastating flood in October 1903, which lasted from October 8–19 and involved the Passaic River and all its tributaries. This followed on the heels of an extremely rainy summer. Dover, N.J. had 15" of rain in June and another 9" in August; Paterson had 11" in June and 11" in August; Newark had 11 1/2" in June and 15" in August. Between October 8 and October 11, 12" of rain fell in thirty-six hours. During the entire period of rain, the amount of water that fell on the Passaic River drainage area equaled 27,273,000 cubic feet. This amount could have covered Central Park to a height of 645' or, at the rate of consumption at the time, could have supplied Newark with water for twenty years. All the bridges on the Passaic River were destroyed. This disaster would certainly have caused massive unemployment.

In October 1903, Giuseppina had three children under the age of 8 and was in the middle of her fifth pregnancy. What hardships she and Angelo must have endured. While the trip back to Italy presented its own hardships, at least at the end of the line, a home was waiting for them. So, sometime between March 1904 and May 1906, they returned to Cordenons, where Renato Belli's future bride, Lydia, was born on May 27, 1906. However, Angelo and Giuseppina never gave up on their dream to live in America. So in March 1910, Angelo took his two sons, John, age 14 and Jack, age 12, and departed for the U.S. once again, leaving behind Giuseppina, their three daughters, and a son, Guido (Bill), who was born on October 12, 1908. In the early 1900s, Angelo's two younger brothers, Osvaldo and Giuseppe, had both visited America. Osvaldo had settled in Park Ridge, N.J. and started a farm, but Giuseppe returned to Cordenons. Aunt Anna writes that Angelo, John, and Jack lived with friends in Clifton. However, the 1910 U.S. Census (April) has them living with Osvaldo in Park Ridge.

Then, Aunt Anna writes, Angelo "became ill and left the boys [in N.J.] so he could go back to Cordenons to see his doctor, where he recovered." This seems a long way to go to see a doctor. But perhaps Angelo's illness was related to his Erb's palsy, and the doctor in Cordenons had been treating him since birth.

Upon learning of the boys' situation, Giuseppina was not happy, so she took matters into her own hands and returned to the U.S. alone. She found work for herself as a weaver, work for John with Richardson Scale in the Athenia section of Clifton, and left Jack with friends of hers in the Delawanna section of Clifton. As she had most likely done earlier, she was probably living in the Botany Village section near the woolen mills.

The family was then separated for the next three years, with Giuseppina, John, and Jack in Clifton, and Angelo, Mary, Anna, Lydia, and Bill in Cordenons.

There is no record of Giuseppina and the boys' time in Clifton. There must have been correspondence, but no letters have survived. Aunt Anna writes extensively of life in Cordenons. Lydia, born in 1906 two years after Anna, was too young to remember very much. However, she must have been happy in Cordenons because, much later, on visits to Italy, she revisited family there and kept in touch with relatives in the U.S., especially Dusolina Ponzo, who lived in Queens, N.Y.

By 1913, Giuseppina must have been well settled in Clifton with a steady job and a place to live. So, finally, Angelo returned to the U.S. and brought the four younger children with him. They sailed from Le Havre on the SS *France*, the fastest ship of the French Line. It was just a year old and nicknamed "The Versailles of the Atlantic" for its opulent decor. Angelo and family, however, no doubt saw little of it as they traveled in steerage. With them on the voyage was a 10-year-old girl from Cordenons whom Angelo was escorting to her parents who were already in America. This is the second time Angelo appears to have accompanied an immigrant from Cordenons to America.[1] Could he have been paid for this service? Even so, it was a kindhearted and generous thing to do.

Soon the family was together at 229 Dayton Avenue, Clifton, N.J. The house is still there. The girls and Guido started school at Clifton's School #7. (It no longer exists, but used to be on Parker Avenue near Sacred Heart Church, which does still exist.) Lydia, then age 7, was placed in kindergarten along with Guido; Anna, age 9, and Mary, age 12, were placed in first grade, probably because of their inability to speak English. Years later, Lydia still remembered being taunted by the other children for this failing. As children will do, they picked up their new language easily; the next year, Mary, Anna, and Lydia were promoted to grades more appropriate.

But just as the young DePieros were beginning to feel at home in their new surroundings, the family moved yet again, this time to Newark, N.J., where Angelo, John, and Jack had found work in a bottling factory. Most likely, this was Consolidated Bottling Company at 329–331 Orange Street. The family lived on Orange Street. Anna, Lydia, and Guido attended Roseville Avenue School. This school still exists. However, the bottling plant soon went bankrupt, and the family moved again, this time to Garfield, N.J. Here Giuseppina could find work as a weaver in the nearby woolen mills. Angelo found a job as a night watchman. Aunt Anna writes that "John found work elsewhere," but is not specific. Jack, on the other hand, joined the U.S. Navy. According to Lydia in later years, Jack had a girlfriend who jilted him. He swore off women and joined the Navy "to see the world," as its slogan went. He headed for France, but WWI got in the

---

1 There is also a record of Angelo entering the U.S. on April 14, 1907 on the SS *Savoie* out of Le Havre, France. With him was a couple from Cordenons. At that time, Angelo was already a U.S. citizen. The couple was immigrating to America, so Angelo might have been accompanying them as a sponsor or just as someone who knew the ropes.

way, and he never saw more of the world. (As for women, Jack never married but never tired of regaling us with stories of his lady friends.)

Chapter 4

Moving to the Country . . . and Education

SOMETIME AFTER THE FAMILY MOVED to Garfield, friends from Cordenons—the DeMarcos—visited Angelo and Giuseppina. The DeMarcos lived in New York City where they had a business on 14th Street, but they wanted to get out of the city and move to the country. Antonio DeMarco knew of a farm in Chatham, N.J., that was for sale. Giuseppina thought that this would be a good move for her and the family, too. She could then realize her dream of taking in boarders to earn money and also be out in the country. So Angelo and Antonio went to view the property and put a down payment on it. Unfortunately, Giuseppina didn't accompany them. When the family arrived there on moving day, she discovered that the house could not accommodate any boarders. But by then the die had been cast. Aunt Anna refers to this as "Mother's first disappointment," which leads one to suspect there were others, but Anna doesn't mention them.

The house was on Myersville Road in Chatham Township. As a child, I remember our family occasionally taking this road to visit Aunt Anna in nearby Gillette, and Lydia would point out the house. It is no longer there. At the Morris County Hall of Records, I did find a copy of the transfer of deed recorded on September 17, 1917. Angelo DePiero and Antonio Demarco bought two parcels of land, one of 5 acres and another of 7 acres from a family named Fries. For these they paid "... One Dollar and other good and valuable considerations, lawful money of the United States of America ..."[2] There is no record of what the "considerations" might have been. When the DePieros moved to Chatham Township, they brought Emma DeMarco, daughter of Antonio, with them. Another act of generosity.

Life on the farm could not have been easy. Angelo must have had difficulty working it with one arm atrophied. Aunt Anna writes that he found work in a florist shop in nearby Murray Hill. The family had no car, so every morning Giuseppina drove him to work with a horse and wagon. Presumably, she had to go back in the evening to bring him home. However, Lydia, then 11, always spoke with affection of her time on the farm. She and Anna and Guido went to the Red Brick Schoolhouse, which is now a museum. The school was almost 3 miles from the farm, so they rode the local school bus, or rather, horse-drawn school wagon. On June 19, 1919, Lydia received a County School Certificate stating that she had completed the prescribed study for the eighth grade in Morris County where Chatham Township is located. Her name is entered as "Lillian" DePiero. When questioned in later years, she had no explanation for this.

At this point, the family must have been struggling to make a go of it on the farm. As Aunt Anna writes: "Mother realized that things were not working out well for us on the farm."[3] There was nowhere for Giuseppina to find work as a weaver

2 Transfer of deed recorded at Morris County Hall of Records.

3 Anna DePiero Turrin, *Remembrances* (Turrin, 1989).

or for the two older girls, Mary and Anna, to find work either. The house would not accommodate any boarders so that avenue of extra income was nonexistent. Shortly after Lydia's completion of eighth grade, the decision was made to return to Clifton. They brought with them the daughter of their neighbor in Chatham, Loretta Kevlin. In Clifton they rented a house at 112 Mahar Avenue. The 1920 census lists Angelo, Giuseppina, Anthony (22), Mary (19), Anna (16), "Lelia" (Lydia, 13), William (Guido, 12) DePiero, and Loretta "Caveline" (Kevlin, 18) as residents there.

Mary and Anthony (Jack) found jobs. Anna and Loretta attended Drake's Business School for a while and then found work as weavers. Lydia and Guido (Bill) continued their schooling, and Lydia completed a two-year commercial course at Clifton High School. On June 24, 1921, she received her diploma which lists the subjects studied and her "academic counts" (credits):

Stenography and Typewriting	15
Bookkeeping and Penmanship	10
English	10
Commercial Arithmetic	5
Physical Training	.2

On her diploma, Lydia's name was, once again, "Lillian." Why were these two mistakes never corrected? Why were they ever made to begin with? These are questions I wish I had known to ask while Lydia was still alive. Perhaps the authorities were trying to make "Lydia" more American. Perhaps the fact that she was an immigrant made Lydia hesitant to speak up and make waves. Whatever the reason, she definitely wanted to assimilate and long remembered the teasing she had received from her fellow elementary school students about her inability to speak English.

After high school, Lydia continued her secretarial studies at Drake's Business School in Passaic. When she'd completed a year's study there, she found a job as a secretary to John Belli, Renato's favorite brother. John was a plumber with an office on Lakeview Avenue, Clifton. Lydia once recalled he was so short that when he sat in the swivel chair at his desk his feet didn't touch the floor. Renato would have visited John at the office, but he and Lydia most likely knew of each other already. Giuseppina's hometown, Borca di Cadore, is adjacent to San Vito di Cadore, Renato's hometown. Both are very small towns, so it is quite possible that the families knew of each other.

Angelo DePiero with children, from left: Lydia, Anna, Mary, and Guido (Bill).

Giuseppina Varettoni DePiero with sons,
from left: Attilio (John) and Antonio (Jack).

The DePiero family c. 1918, from left: Anna, Angelo, Jack, Lydia, Bill, John, Giuseppina, and Mary.

Lydia, April 21, 1924.

Lydia, Giuseppina, and Anna. From the private collection of Jen DePiero Kimball.

Giuseppina's handwoven sheet.

Lydia's elementary school in Chatham, N.J.

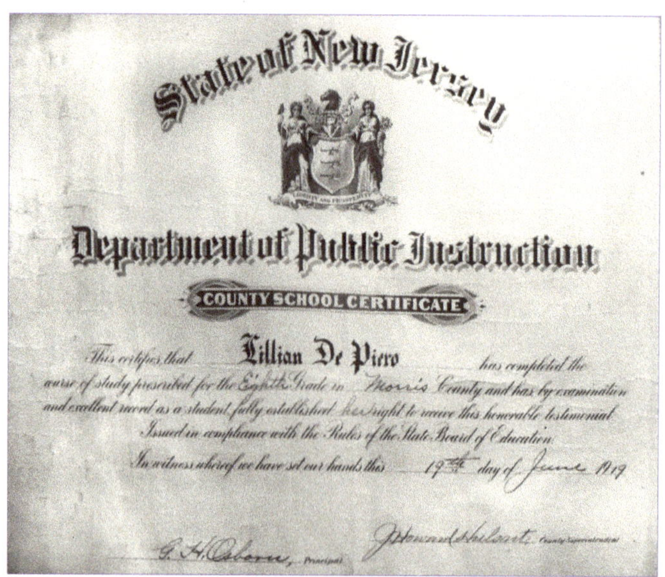

State of New Jersey

Department of Public Instruction

COUNTY SCHOOL CERTIFICATE

This certifies that Lillian De Piero has completed the course of study prescribed for the Eighth Grade in Morris County and has by examination and excellent record as a student fully established her right to receive this honorable testimonial.

Issued in compliance with the Rules of the State Board of Education.

In witness whereof we have set our hands this 19th day of June 1919

G. H. Osborne, Principal

J. Howard Hulsart, County Superintendent

Lydia's elementary school diploma.

Clifton High School

BOARD OF EDUCATION
CLIFTON, NEW JERSEY

Certificate

This certifies that Lillian De Piero
has satisfactorily completed the two-year Commercial course
in this School with the following academic counts:

English	10	General Science		Local industries	
German		Algebra		Commercial Geography	
French		Commercial Arithmetic	5	History of Commerce	
Spanish		Bookkeeping and Penmanship	10	Mechanical Drawing	
History		Stenography and Typewriting	15	Freehand Drawing	
Biology		Commercial Law		Physical Training	2

Date [illegible]

[illegible]
PRESIDENT OF THE BOARD OF EDUCATION

Lydia's high school diploma.

DePiero house in Cordenons, Italy.

CHAPTER 5

The Belli Family

RENATO BELLI WAS BORN in San Vito di Cadore on February 22, 1897. He was the son of Tiziano (July 12, 1848–1926) and Dorotea DeSandre Belli (December 5, 1857–April 1, 1925), and the third of their thirteen children to be born on February 22—Giuseppe, the oldest, was born on February 22, 1883, and Alba, later a nun, was born on February 22, 1892.

Like the DePieros, the Bellis were a well-established family in their town. The family tree dates back to the thirteenth century, and one member named Jacopo in the fourteenth century was called *al bel* (Handsome Jake, probably a nickname). Jacopo's son was known as Pietro del (son of) Bel, and so was born the surname Del Bel or Belli. In the fifteenth century, the family moved from the Chiapuzza neighborhood of San Vito to the neighborhood of Serdes where some of the family still lives today. There were many families with the name Belli in Serdes. "Around the end of the [seventeenth] century, a certain Giovanni Battista Belli was nicknamed Zan (dialect for Gian), and his children were called Belli DeZan (of John) to distinguish them from Bellis to whom they were not related. A generation later, another Giovanni Belli de

Zan was nicknamed 'Traculeta' (one who staggers) [perhaps he was lame or perhaps he drank a bit too much?], and his children were called 'I Traculetes' (the staggerers). One of these children, Pietro Belli Traculeta, was the youngest of [twelve] and was nicknamed 'al Codan,' that is to say, the 'tail end.' And his descendants were called 'I Codanes.' This same Pietro Codan was the grandfather of Bepo Codan, who was the father of Tiziano 'Rosso' (for his red hair) Codan who was the father of Renato."[4]

Life in the little mountain town of San Vito was hard, and as a very young man, Tiziano began traveling throughout Europe to find work as a carpenter. He was quite skilled at constructing the framework for bridges as attested to by this description of his work on a German railroad.

Certificate of Merit

> To Master Builder Tiziano Belli from San Vito di Cadore, prov. Venezia, now residing in Oberbeisheim (Germany) and present here, it is sworn at his request that from April 1877 until today he has been employed in these construction sites for the building of the State Railway Berlin-Coblenz. During this time, Mr. Belli, with his team, helped to build and install all the frameworks for the FZ viaduct 30m. high with iron facing and 6 vaults of 32m.
>
> After the completion of the viaduct, Mr. Belli obtained from the wood used some planks for the Kamfeld tunnel and some beams for the parapets and installed them.

4 Don Aldo Belli, "A Short History of the Family of Giuseppe and of Tiziano (Rosso) Belli Codan," 1976.

> Mr. Belli is a skilled and diligent carpenter and can with every right be considered a resolute and upright man.
>
> Hamberg, January 8, 1879

Tiziano spent almost two years at this job. His German must have been quite good when he finished, and the work must have been quite lucrative. He continued traveling even after marrying, and family history has it that he would return home with his pockets full of gold coins.

By the time he was age 50, Tiziano had five sons: Giuseppe (1883–1959), Giovanni (1886–1928), Cesare (1888–1939), Luigi (1889–1969), and Renato (1897–1987). He also had three daughters: Giovanna (1891–1926), Alba (1892–197?), Maria (1895–1918), as well as two daughters who had died: Giovanna (1884–1886) and Teresa (1895–1895). At that time, there were also three sons yet to come: Albino (1899–1971), Arturo (1900–1968), and Ottavio (1904–1905).

Well used to traveling, but perhaps tired of being away from home so often, and with no means to support his family well in San Vito, Tiziano decided to bring his family to America. In 1901, he took Giovanni, Cesare, and Luigi and traveled to New York on the SS *Aquitaine* from Le Havre, arriving on January 21, 1901. They then proceeded to Clifton, N.J., to stay with a sister of Tiziano, Teresa Belli Marmoci. He found work for his sons in a factory and, for himself, as a carpenter. After two years, he returned alone to San Vito with the intention of bringing the rest of the family to America. However, Dorotea, who was now 47 and had never ventured outside of San Vito, didn't feel up to leaving Italy and going to a new world. In addition, shortly after Tiziano returned, his mother, *Bisnonna* (Great-grandmother) Giovanna, passed away, and he inherited a house to live in and the gristmill, which gave him the means to support his family. He decided to remain in Italy, thereby splitting the family in two.

Renato, age 7, was now the oldest of the boys at home with three older sisters and two younger brothers. He was a little young to be expected to assume much responsibility, but by age 10 he was required to forsake school in order to help Tiziano run his business. Some of this involved a horse that Renato rose at 4:00 a.m. to feed and make ready to pull the wagons of other families. For the rest of his life, he felt the lack of more formal education, but he was always ready to learn. He learned to read and write easily in both Italian and English, and his penmanship was beautiful. In 1921, his command of English was good enough for him to take correspondence courses in engineering from the International Correspondence School.

CHAPTER 6

Renato Belli Comes to America

ALTHOUGH THE FAMILY was separated by an ocean, every so often, one of the young men in America would come back to visit his parents and siblings in San Vito. This continued until World War I. If any of them had returned to Italy during the war, they would have been conscripted. After the war, if any returned they would have been arrested as deserters.

In 1910 or 1911, it was Luigi's turn to travel to Italy. Upon arrival, he was wearing a pair of high button shoes; when Renato saw them, he decided he had to come to America to get a pair for himself. He had to wait a few years to prepare himself, but by 1914, at age 17, he was ready. He was a bit uneasy about asking his father for permission, so he asked his mother to do it for him. Permission was granted; he sailed from Le Havre, France, on the SS *Rochambeau* and arrived in New York on April 18, 1914.

Many years later he told me a story. When he wrote to his brothers in America that he was coming, Luigi offered to meet him in New York. However, upon arrival, Renato needed to be processed through Ellis Island. There he was asked what his destination was, and he said Clifton, N.J., so the authorities put him on a ferry to Hoboken, N.J., on the opposite side of the

Hudson River from New York City. He arrived there at night completely lost, unable to speak a word of English, and scared. He told me he walked up and down the street calling out in Italian for help. Finally a man who spoke Italian arrived. He took Renato to the train station, bought him a ticket to Clifton and put him on the train. He strongly cautioned him to not give the ticket to anyone, or he might be put off the train. The conductor arrived and asked for his ticket. Renato was determined not to surrender it, and a heated argument ensued, probably due to the inability of each of them to speak the other's language. Another passenger, Italian, managed to settle the impasse. That stranger turned out to be the next-door neighbor of Renato's brother, Cesare, and he escorted Renato the rest of the way.

Before he had left San Vito, Renato's sister, Maria, made him a cloth wallet, which she had hand embroidered. Inside, she pinned a tiny-framed photograph of herself and one of Tiziano. I doubt that Renato ever used it, but he kept it for the rest of his life. As Giuseppina's sheet is for the DePieros, this wallet is for the Bellis. A powerful, tangible connection to our roots. It also must have had great sentimental value for Renato because Maria, older than Renato by two years, had died at age 23 during WWI. As the Austrian troops were retreating in November 1918, they passed through San Vito looking for all the supplies they could find. Three soldiers arrived at the Belli residence and confiscated some butter. They also wanted to confiscate Maria. She tried to fight them off to no avail. Tiziano announced he would kill her rather than let her go with the Austrians. Dorotea convinced them that Maria would only be a hindrance to their flight, so they left. Maria was terrified they would return, so she hid overnight under the water wheel that ran the gristmill. From the cold and the damp, she developed pneumonia and died two weeks later.

As a young boy in Italy, Renato had been trained to be a blacksmith to go along with his responsibilities for the horse. He also, assuredly, learned carpentry skills from Tiziano. There being less of a call in the U.S. for blacksmiths now that cars were taking over the roads from horses, Renato looked for work as a carpenter. One of his first jobs was working on the New York subway station at Herald Square in Manhattan. For this job he lived in a fleabag hotel in New York and subsisted on doughnuts. One day, a hammer he was using slipped out of his hand, landed on the head of another worker below him, and knocked him unconscious. Afraid the man might have been killed, Renato fled the scene and never returned. Another early job was laying floors in a Remington munitions factory in Bridgeport, Connecticut. So he continued the example set by Tiziano of traveling to find work.

In 1917, the United States entered WWI, and a military draft was instituted. All males of a certain age were required to register. However, an immigrant who was not yet a citizen could claim an exemption called the "alienage exemption." This exempted him from military duty but prohibited him from ever applying for citizenship. At this point, Renato was age 20 and a prime candidate for the draft. That he applied for the exemption is evident from his application for citizenship in 1924. It notes that he had previously applied for citizenship in 1921, and that it had been denied because of the "alienage exemption . . . and [that] the cause of such denial has since been cured or removed." How did this happen? Shortly after the U.S. Congress passed the alienage exemption law, they passed another law granting exemption to anyone working at a job that was essential to the war effort—and they made it retroactive. Renato and his brothers were working in the Hoboken Navy Yard, and so they were exempt. Renato may have previously applied for the alienage exemption but was now exempt, thus allowing him to apply for citizenship after the war. However, one still wonders why this information wasn't available in 1921 when Renato declared his intention of applying for citizenship. Nevertheless, on November 24, 1924, Renato Belli filed a petition for naturalization with the Court of Common Pleas in Paterson, N.J. His witnesses were Romolo Marmoci, a first cousin, and John Belli, Renato's brother, with whom he lived at 81 Lakeview Ave., Clifton. His petition was granted on April 23, 1925, following his oath of allegiance to the U.S.

Cousin Roy Belli told me that when the brothers were working in the Hoboken Shipyard in New Jersey and learned that due to their jobs they were exempt from the draft, they celebrated by going out and getting drunk. The next morning they were late to work and were fired, but they must have managed to talk their way back into their jobs.

CHAPTER 7

Post-WWI

AFTER THE WAR, Renato continued to travel to find work. In 1919, he was living in Poughkeepsie, N.Y., and in 1921, he was living in Trenton, N.J. By 1922, he was back in Clifton and living with his brother John.

The Italian American Family Association of Botany Village, Clifton, was formed in 1909. One of its functions was as a food cooperative. It became a thriving business, and in 1924, it was able to erect its own building on Parker Avenue in Botany Village, Clifton. Bids were solicited for its construction. Having already formed Belli Construction Company and built a few private homes, Renato entered the competition. His bid turned out to be the lowest, winning him the job. He completed the job on time and under budget with a profit of $20,000. The building is still standing. A bar and grocery store are on the ground floor; the second floor boasts two-storeys-high Palladian windows, a ballroom, stage, and kitchen and bar facilities. The food cooperative is no more, but the Italian American Family Association still exists. They rent out their hall and do a thriving catering business on most weekends.

Renato was now financially able to buy himself a car. He chose a Pierce–Arrow, a luxury car of the early to mid-twentieth century. What model he chose has not been recorded, but one 1924 model included an 8-cylinder engine and 4-wheel brakes. There is no record of him taking driving lessons, which likely contributed to his reputation for minor scrapes. Or maybe they were not so minor. According to family legend, he once hit a trolley car and pushed it off the tracks. Another time he ended up with the long hood of his car under the back end of a paint truck. Lydia always said he drove "like a cowboy."

Tiziano Belli

Dorotea DeSandre Belli

Belli family in San Vito, Italy, c. 1907. Seated: Dorotea and Tiziano; standing in front, left to right: Renato, Arturo, Albino; standing in back, left to right: Giovanna, Alba, and Maria.

San Vito di Cadore

Renato's birthplace.

The house on the Boite River where Renato grew up, c. 1900.

The house on the Boite, c. 2010.

Renato's fourth-grade class. He is standing alone in the third row on the left.

The wallet that Renato's sister, Maria, made for him when he left for America in 1914.

The wallet with photos of Tiziano and Maria.

Renato, c. 1920.

Cooperative Hall nearing completion in 1924.

Stage in ballroom of Cooperative Hall. Renato is pictured at left with the painter. Renato was extremely proud of the artwork.

By 1922, Lydia had finished high school and business school and had found a job with Renato's brother John. She also worked for a while for an architect who sometimes sent her to New York City to deliver blueprints. This involved taking the train to Hoboken and the ferry to Manhattan. The ferry docked at Chambers Street at the extreme lower end of the island. Not trusting herself to the subway, Lydia would walk from there to her destination near Times Square, a distance of 3 1/2 miles. Naturally, she had to walk back to Chambers Street to get the ferry back to Hoboken. Quite a trek through what was the not best part of the city.

So Renato and Lydia connected at his brother John's office on Lakeview Avenue. Or reconnected, since their families probably knew each other. Renato would have known Lydia, but because she was nine years younger than he was, he wouldn't have considered her dating material earlier. At any rate, he was now smitten; he invited Lydia to a dance at the Majestic Boat Club in Carlstadt, N.J., where he was a member. She was then 16 and he, 25. They didn't return from the dance until 6:00 a.m. Their story, which never varied in the forty-five years I knew them, was that they had missed the last trolley from Carlstadt and had to wait all night for another one. Giuseppina was livid and forbade them another date for six months. After that, their courtship continued for four more years and culminated in their marriage at 10:00 a.m. on October 2, 1926 in Sacred Heart RC Church in Clifton.

After a short honeymoon, Renato and Lydia set up housekeeping at 111 Bergen Avenue, Clifton. This was a two-family house built by Belli Construction Company. Renato and Lydia lived on the second floor, the *piano nobile* (noble floor) of homes in Italy that housed more than one family.

The first floor was rented to a family called Jolly. A driveway ran alongside of the house leading to a three-car garage with a second storey that was equipped as a carpenter's workshop. This workshop was often full of sawdust, and the smell of it even now brings back my childhood. Only two cars were ever housed in the garage. The third space had a separate door and was used for storage of bicycles, sleds, snow shovels, and anything else too cumbersome to carry upstairs. I don't remember anything of the second floor apartment because by the time I was born, the family had moved down to the first floor, and new tenants occupied the second. They were the Hankins family: Clarence, Harriet, and Harriet's son by a previous marriage, Sammy Sanders. Aunt Harriet, as David and I called her, worked in a hair salon. When I was 1 year old, she began giving me manicures and painting my fingernails. This lasted until my little brother, David, was born, and she fell in love with him and abandoned me, to my great annoyance. To this day I do not manicure.

Chapter 8

Renato and Lydia's Children and Traditions

AS I NOTED BEFORE, Renato and Lydia's first child, Florence Vivian, arrived on September 13, 1927. She was followed by William Renato on June 13, 1930. In between, in 1929, Renato and Lydia had welcomed into their home three of Renato's brother Cesare's children, as their mother, Katie, had passed away from tuberculosis. They stayed until Cesare was able to care for them and their younger sister in their house on Hamilton Avenue, Clifton. That same year saw the beginning of the Great Depression. Times were difficult, but Renato worked hard to support the family. He often reminded us that he carried coal on his back to do so. He also worked for the WPA (Works Progress Administration), established in 1935. This work included building schools. These included the Midland School in Rochelle Park, N.J., and Thomas Jefferson High School (now the middle school) in Lodi, N.J. Both are still standing. By sheer coincidence, Anthony Piacentini, future husband of Renato's granddaughter Lydia, attended the Lodi school. From one school Renato brought home a piece of leftover slate and made a blackboard with a chalk rail, which he hung in the basement. Every day I would come home from school and pretend to teach. I had no students, but it was good practice for the future.

Towards the end of the depression, Renato developed severe sciatica. He was unable to walk around the block to visit his brother Joe without great pain. He saw doctors at Columbia Presbyterian Hospital in New York. They recommended amputating his leg. Thoroughly shocked, he returned home to celebrate Thanksgiving and consider the surgery, which would have severely impacted his ability to continue as a builder. He chose instead to become the patient of a chiropractor in nearby Bloomfield. He continued to see him for ten years until he was completely cured. As a little girl, I remember being cautioned not to sit on his right leg when I sat on his lap. But in later years, I don't remember him ever complaining of sciatic pain.

Lydia was a thrifty homemaker. In 1934, she kept a detailed list of household expenses. These were mostly for food but they also recorded expenditures for clothes, entertainment, doctors, insurance, and so on. In May there's a $34.00 payment to the dentist. This is a huge bill when a dozen eggs cost $.35 and a doctor's visit was $5.00. It might have been for Renato's full set of dentures. Insurance was probably life insurance and cost $5.00/month (the biggest lump sum monthly expenditure). Entertainment includes the movies at $.35 and a trip to New York's Radio City Music Hall: $1.70 for transportation and $1.20 for tickets. Renato always thought Radio City was the cat's pajamas. But there was no live theatre for him unless it was the occasional performance at the Metropolitan Opera when it was still on 39th St. The shows' librettos were kept for years. Every week Lydia paid $1.50 for Florence to take dancing lessons, tap and acrobatic: tap shoes cost $.50, and there's a $3.00 deposit on a costume, so there must have been a recital. Every so often there's an additional expenditure for "private dancing." Were Lydia and Renato taking ballroom dancing lessons? They were both good dancers in later years.

Money was also spent at the Cooperative, i.e., the Italian American Family Association on Parker Avenue. Purchases there are not itemized so perhaps Renato was making them. He was the one with a car at his disposal, and he may have purchased in quantity. These averaged $25.00 per month.

Lastly, in July 1934, Lydia entered $92.50 for a two-week vacation. There is no indication of where they went, but just the fact that they were able to go indicates an adequate income. Renato was not one for vacations, so perhaps Lydia took Florence and Bill away somewhere.

Lydia continues the record for 1935, and expenditures have almost doubled. Renato must have started work for the WPA as soon as it came into effect. In February 1935, a piano was purchased for $22.00. This was an upright player piano, but the player mechanism was eventually removed. Both Florence and I took lessons on it, and it remained in the family until the late 1980s. On May 30, there was another trip to Radio City Music Hall, probably in honor of Lydia's birthday, which was May 27. The show cost $1.20, and dinner for three (?) cost $1.65 with a $0.15 tip. Expenses for gas and electric ($14.65 for 2 mos.) and telephone ($7.45) are included, but they are listed with Cooperative expenses so Renato was probably paying these also. Lydia's yearly total of expenses for 1935 is almost twice as high as that for 1934.

By 1935, Florence and Bill were both in school, and Lydia became involved in their experience. She was an active member of the PTA of School No. 11, Clifton. Her organizational ability (passed down from Giuseppina) and her ability to motivate must have been greatly appreciated. In future years, she went on to hold office in the local PTA, and at some point was asked to run for election to the state organization. This would have involved regular travel to New Jersey's capital, Trenton, and time spent away from home. Renato was not in favor, so Lydia acquiesced. But she did leave us an example of her participation. I found the following introductory speech written out fully in longhand in the back of her expenses notebook of 1934–1935:

> On behalf of all the Parent Teacher Associations of Clifton, I am very happy to welcome you here tonight. For one who has been interested in Parent-Teacher work for some time, I am happy to see how well this movement is progressing in our city. It is with the combined efforts of the home and school that we can expect to do our best in the education of our children and in helping them to meet life's complex problems.
>
> I wish to thank each president of our P.T.A.s who has helped to make it possible to sponsor this evening. I also wish to thank the principals of all our schools for their interest and cooperation. I regret that Mr. Smith, our superintendent, could not be with us tonight to introduce our speaker.
>
> But in turning the meeting over to Mr. Staub, principal of School No. 11, I am presenting to you a man sincerely interested in the education of our children, a man deeply enthusiastic about his work, a man who has the welfare of the children at heart, Mr. Staub, who will introduce our guest speaker.

Her advancement in the PTA thwarted, Lydia found another way to satisfy her desire to do good. She joined the Cordial Women's Club. The club was founded in 1934, so Lydia may well have been one of its founders. Its members were dedicated to helping those less fortunate. These were mostly Clifton residents, but I also remember accompanying Lydia on visits to the Little Sisters of the Poor in Paterson. The Cordial Women, who lived up to their name, met once a month in Botany Village, and I doubt that Lydia ever missed a meeting. Eventually she became president for several years. The *Herald News* announced that at the June 16, 1951 meeting of the Cordial Women's Club, "Mrs. Rene [*sic*] Belli was re-elected president."

To raise funds for their good works, the ladies held an annual pre-Thanksgiving dance at the Cooperative Hall, the same Cooperative Hall built by Renato. In 1954, there were five hundred attendees. It must have been the highlight of the social season in Botany Village. The women ran the kitchen and their husbands ran the bar. Of course there was a band that played polkas, waltzes, fox trots, cha-chas, and more. Renato and Lydia were good dancers. Where they learned has not been recorded unless that entry for "dancing" in Lydia's expense record indicates lessons for them. A raffle, which included food baskets and turkeys, was held. All the members' families were expected to attend. I remember going at the age of 11 or 12 and other children my age were there, too. It must have been a special occasion, because I was allowed to stay up until 2:00 a.m.

The Cordial Women also held an annual Christmas Party for children, complete with Santa Claus handing out gifts. This also involved good food and lots of games. In addition to these activities there were theatre trips—*Fanny* in 1955, and *My Fair Lady* in 1959—card parties, a 4th annual spaghetti dinner in 1959, and an annual picnic in 1956 at Belli Acres in Saddle River, N.J.

When the family moved to Saddle River in late September 1951, Lydia volunteered in the kitchen of the Valley Hospital café, was a Cub Scout den mother, and taught my Girl Scout troop how to embroider. In 1954, she liked to watch a daytime TV quiz program called *Strike It Rich*. Contestants came on the program, explained their need to "Strike It Rich," and then played a game to win money. One day she learned of the plight of a group of Italian Boy Scouts who had come to New York to visit and were in need of funds. She called the program's "heart line" and invited the boys to dinner at our home. This involved not just dinner but also driving the boys from and to the YMCA where they were staying in New York. I bet a donation was also included.

All during the Great Depression, Angelo and Giuseppina continued to reside at 112 Mahar Avenue, Clifton. Sometime before 1930, they were able to purchase the house, which was valued at $8,000. It was, and is, a big house with room for Angelo, Giuseppina, Jack, Mary and her children, Warren and Dorothy, and more. In 1922, Anna had married Anthony Turrin, and they bought a chicken and egg farm in Gillette, N.J. Mary and children spent a good amount of time on the farm. This gave Giuseppina the opportunity to realize her dream and take in boarders. The 1940 census shows that she had four boarders, all male.

CHAPTER 9

World War II Years . . . Followed by a New House

ON DECEMBER 7, 1941, the United States was greatly surprised by the unexpected attack of the Japanese on Pearl Harbor. Shortly before that, on September 27, Renato and Lydia had been greatly surprised by the unexpected arrival of me. Well, not totally unexpected in September, but up until three months before, Lydia had insisted she had a tumor. Perhaps she felt uncomfortable revealing the truth. At that time in the U.S., it was unusual for a woman of her age (35) to have a child, especially if she had two older children the younger of which was 11. Be that as it may, Lydia and Renato must have been overjoyed at my arrival because two years later they had another child, this time a boy, David. When I arrived they moved down to the first floor of 111 Bergen Ave., and there they remained until 1951.

Sometime during the 1940s and possibly at its founding in 1941, Renato became associated with Center Savings and Loan of Clifton. He sat on the board of directors and did appraisals of properties for which mortgages were pending. He was rightly proud of this position and continued to attend meetings into his 80s . . . and if anyone in the family needed a mortgage for a new home, they went to Center Savings. As a director, Renato was entitled to a four-day paid trip once a year to Atlantic City, N.J., for the state Savings and Loan Association convention. Wives were included. Renato and Lydia never missed a trip.

Also during the 1940s, David and I started school, and Florence and Bill graduated from high school. Bill went off to Eastern Baptist Seminary in Philadelphia, and Florence entered Bethany College in West Virginia, a small school with a total enrollment of nine hundred. Bethany was a town so small that when he first visited, Renato drove straight through without realizing it. For her senior year, Florence decided to go to a larger school, and she chose the University of California at Berkeley. Her graduating class alone numbered two thousand. At Christmas, she was offered her choice between a plane ticket home and a fur jacket. She chose the jacket and spent New Year's Day in Pasadena at the Rose Parade. For her graduation, Renato, Lydia, and Bill drove to California. On the way they stopped in Las Vegas and bought David and me cowboy and cowgirl outfits. The owner of the shop was named Belli, but of Swiss origin. Renato made a point of mentioning that his father had built bridges in Switzerland, implying that they might be related. The owner replied, "I had a mother, but I also had a father." The outfits were sent back to New Jersey intended as Christmas presents. When the package arrived, David and I were thrilled . . . chaps/skirt, vest, and boots. The letter advising us not to open until Christmas arrived the next day.

In later years when Renato was leaving for a construction site in his pickup truck, he would let me ride to the end of the driveway on the running board. I would always ask, "Where are you going?" The answer was always the same: "To California!"

In addition to wanting to help those less fortunate, Lydia was very civic minded. She was proud of her American citizenship, which she received, even though she was born in Italy, automatically at birth because her father was already a U.S. citizen. She took her civic responsibilities seriously and was the only person I've ever known who complained to her congressman, a neighbor, that she had never been called for jury duty. He fixed that. While she wasn't a card-carrying member of a political party, she was certain to vote when required. How she voted was never revealed, but as a good wife of the mid-twentieth century, she may have followed Renato's lead and voted Republican; or, since the vote was secret, she may have exercised her independence. It would be fun to know.

Baby parades became popular at the Jersey shore during the early 1900s. Infants and toddlers were paraded in carriages and strollers along the boardwalk. Asbury Park had its first in 1890; Ocean City had its first in 1909 and its 110th in 2019. They were a way of promoting a city and of encouraging its citizens to work together. Baby parades must have appealed to Lydia because in the late 1940s she organized more than one in Clifton. And she made them more than just an unending procession of babies and toddlers. Each parade had a Queen, the academically highest-ranking female of the most recent graduating class of Clifton High School. The Queen rode on a large float that carried another ten or twelve high school girls (princesses) and two pages. The Queen wore a long robe with a train, so train bearers were required. Lydia recruited me to be one. At the end of the parade route, the Queen came down from the float, ascended onto a platform, and recited a memorized speech. Ergo, the need for train bearers. The speech was probably a quote from Shakespeare's *A Midsummer Night's Dream.* I remember that because I listened to the Queen rehearse her lines, and it was the first time I ever heard the name "Titania." Not your run-of-the-mill baby parade. Not when organized by Lydia DePiero

Belli. In 1949, 5-year-old David, wearing his Las Vegas cowboy outfit, rode a pony in the parade.

One night, Giuseppina came to babysit David and me. After we were in bed, she went out to buy us ice cream cones. At that time, Clifton was a safe enough city for her to be able to leave us alone; or maybe she asked Aunt Harriet upstairs to keep an eye on us. She only had to walk a half block to the corner, turn right, and walk another half block to LaManna's candy store. The cones and ice cream were sold separately, the ice cream being individual MelloRolls, cylinders of ice cream wrapped in paper. When Giuseppina returned, she stayed in the kitchen to put the ice cream in the cones. This was not an easy task as the diameter of the roll was almost the same as that of the cone. One of the rolls must have missed its mark and fallen on the table. Giuseppina let out an "Awww, shit." Though we were in our bedroom, David and I heard her and had a hard time stifling our giggling. We knew that she would not be pleased to hear us laughing at her.

Angelo passed away on November 1, 1942. He was 76 years old and is buried in Calvary Cemetery in Clifton. I have no memory of him, and I cherish the photo of me with him and Giuseppina that was taken shortly before he died. Giuseppina continued to live in the house on Mahar Avenue for a few years and then sold it and moved to the farm in Gillette.

David in the 1949 Clifton Baby Parade.

The house Renato built in 1924 where he and Lydia lived after they were married.

John DePiero with Angelo, c. 1930. From the private collection of Jen DePiero Kimball.

Angelo with John's wife, Anna, and granddaughter, Jen, July 4, 1930. From the private collection of Jen DePiero Kimball.

Angelo with Giuseppina, holding Lynn.

Clifton Baby Parade, 1949.

Giuseppina; Lydia's daughter, Florence; and Lydia, c. 1941.

By the late 1940s, the house at 111 Bergen Avenue had become too small for Renato and Lydia and their children. The floor they occupied consisted of a living room, dining room, kitchen, one bathroom, two average size bedrooms, and one tiny bedroom that only could be reached by walking through one of the other ones. An extra bedroom had been built in the attic for Bill. After having graduated from college, Florence was now living at home while she worked in Paterson.

So with Renato's construction business booming after the war, he and Lydia decided to build another home. Every Sunday they took a drive "looking for property." Lydia, as usual, wanted the best they could afford. Around this same time she made the acquaintance of Sam and Raffie Jenco through one of Renato's nieces. The Jencos had just built a house in Saddle River. When Lydia saw Saddle River, she decided it was for her. It was quite suburban and a more upscale community than Clifton. Her eye, and probably also the eye of an agent, led her to the choicest piece of property along Chestnut Ridge Road—the highest point on the ridge. (Even though the house was never air-conditioned, it always had a cooling breeze.) Renato and Lydia bought 7 acres of land for their new home.

For a long time Lydia had known who the architect would be. Arthur Rigolo, who later went on to win many awards for his designs, was a close neighbor in Clifton. Also, his mother was from San Vito, a connection that must have pleased Renato. After graduating from the University of Illinois in 1934, Rigolo had been associated with several different firms and most recently in partnership with another architect. In 1948, he started his own firm. Lydia's eye for the best did not disappoint her. However, she also had definite ideas of what she wanted in the house. These must have caused Rigolo to alter his original plans. Besides, Renato with his construction experience certainly had opinions about materials. These, too, may have caused Rigolo to rework things. While clearing out Lydia's desk after her death, I found the following letter:

May 3, 1951

Mr. R. Belli
111 Bergen Ave.
Clifton, N.J.

Dear Mr. Belli,

Enclosed is my bill for services rendered for your house in Saddle River. I am disappointed that the plans for your house would cost so much and frankly it is quite a lot of money to spend on plans for a house. I had originally intended to make you a good set of plans and specifications for about $500.00, but as it turned out, you have a poor set of plans for much more.

Unfortunately the amount billed does not represent a profit for me. My records show 580 1/4 hours spent on this project and since my actual cost is $4.00 per hour, my total cost for this project is $2,321.00. If it will make you feel any better about this, I will be happy to stop up to your project occasionally on Sundays, see you at my leisure moments at any time to discuss any problems, or do so also by telephone. From now on in there will be no charge for this service because it will be rendered as a neighborly favor.

Yours truly,
ARTHUR RIGOLO

A bill was attached:

For professional services rendered . . $2,300.00

In 2020 dollars this comes to $23,000. A princely sum.

Renato might have hit the ceiling when he received this bill, but he would have realized that the hours had been spent and must be paid. And Rigolo's offer not to charge for any future consultations was generous. Lydia, whose very hands-on approach might have incurred these charges, would have kept her mouth shut. Indeed, when the house was finished, it was a prime example of 1950s contemporary design. It was a well laid out ranch style and easy to live in. As one of the few contemporary homes in Saddle River, it became a favorite of real estate agents who regularly appeared to try to convince Lydia and Renato to sell. (They resisted for twenty-five years.)

Construction began in the spring of 1951 and continued through the summer. Renato, of course, was in charge and handpicked the subcontractors who all did an excellent job. In twenty-five years there was never a clogged drain, an electrical problem, or a complaint about a carpenter's work. Renato built things to last (witness the Cooperative Hall which is almost 100 years old), but "graceful" was not part of his vocabulary. So Lydia kept close watch. One of the things she insisted about was the front door knob. Arthur Rigolo had specified a very large circular knob, like one he also used in his own house in Clifton where he positioned it to the side of the door where the knob usually goes.

Lydia must have thought hers would look better in the center of the door, so she had the master carpenter change its position. The carpenter complained that he had to buy a new, extra long drill bit in order to install the lock. But it does look better in the center. However, little changes can add to the total cost. Construction began at the end of March 1951.

Local artist's rendering of the house at 18 Chestnut Ridge Road, Saddle River, N.J., which was nicknamed "Belli Acres."

Giuseppina, c. early 1950s.

Patio that Renato refused to cover in 1953.

Christmas 1965. Front door with the centered doorknob.

Lydia and Renato on their 20th wedding anniversary, October 1946.

In San Vito, many homes have wood paneled parlors, and Renato's early life may well have been spent in one. For the house in Saddle River he handpicked panels of Philippine mahogany for the living room, dining room, and front hallway. They created a warm feeling not possible with paint.

A raised fireplace with a marble hearth was in the living room. This idea is also present in Rigolo's own home, but Renato did him one better. He wanted another raised fireplace in the family room. (Another change Rigolo probably didn't include in his first plans.) This second fireplace allowed Renato to make polenta; from an overhead beam, he hung a chain with a hook on the end to hold the pot while he waited for the water to boil, or so he could take a rest when stirring the polenta. He had grown up in Italy on polenta made over an open fire. To him this was the only proper way to make it—not on a stove, and only in a copper pot. Renato couldn't boil water, but he could make a perfect polenta, which was *de rigeur* on Christmas Eve and at family picnics. (He passed this skill on to his son, David; the tradition still continues and will continue, I hope, for generations.)

During the summer of 1951, Renato was busy overseeing not only the construction of their new home but also the construction of 200 Cape Cod style houses in Cedar Grove, N.J. Lydia was busy buying new furniture, choosing carpeting, doing everything necessary to furnish 18 Chestnut Ridge Road. We now had our first television, our first clothes dryer, our first dishwasher. The dishwasher was only to be run when it was full, but one meal never used enough dishes, and Lydia didn't like to know that dirty dishes were sitting around (even though one couldn't see them). So basically we never used the dishwasher. The clothes dryer took some getting used to, too. On more than one occasion Lydia tossed a wet woolen sweater into it . . . "for just a bit" . . . with the inescapable result. And it did no good to starch crinolines (a 1950's staple) and then put them in the dryer. They came out limp.

Lydia was given free rein when it came to purchases for the house unless the cost came to a lot more than the usual. Then, like a good Italian 1950's wife, she sought Renato's approval. His first reaction was always, "You want to spend how much?! To buy what?! What are you, crazy?!"

Sometimes he relented. She did get the gold leaf cocktail table. But she never got the Mercedes, or the window boxes, or the canopy over the patio.

By the end of September 1951, construction was finished, and we moved in. At that time, Saddle River was a world away from Clifton. Clifton had sidewalks, car traffic, nearby schools, shops within walking distance, and playmates across the street. Saddle River had no sidewalks, little traffic, an elementary school 2 1/2 miles away, no shops except for a drugstore, a deli, and a gas station, and no playmates closer than 3 miles. This meant big changes, especially for those of us who couldn't drive. Mail was not delivered but had to be picked up at the post office in the center of town. The nearest Catholic church was St. Luke's in neighboring Ho-Ho-Kus. There was no police force, only Marshall Wilkes—a real marshall, just like in the westerns we watched on TV. There was no school bus because the law required the school to be more than 3 miles away for a bus to be provided. However, there was a school bus that picked up students to be transported to the regional high school in Ramsey, and sometimes the driver allowed David and me to ride as far as the elementary school in Saddle River. Otherwise, Lydia drove us in the morning and picked us up in the afternoon. But there were times when we walked the 2 1/2 miles home. Not a lot of pampering for us children of immigrants.

Our house was about 400' from Chestnut Ridge Road at the top of a very slight incline. The driveway split the front yard almost exactly in two and ended in a circular section. This section included a carport (a popular 1950's idea) that extended from the front wall of the house, and a small parking area. Behind the house there was a large yard the full length of the house and about 30' wide. The area around the house was seeded as lawn, but a large part of the front area was not. The lawn part needed to be cut with a lawnmower, so Renato purchased a motorized one. However, for the front part that was not seeded, he decided what was needed were two sheep. These would eat any growth close to the ground. Saddle River being so rural he must have wanted to feel like he was back in San Vito.

Two sheep were shortly purchased. These were not cute little lambs as in Mother Goose, but two full-grown, rather ugly ewes. Renato had never tended sheep, so this became a learning experience. The rest of us graciously allowed him to learn by himself.

At night, Renato housed them in a tool shed, but during the day they were in the front yard, which had no fencing. The family next door owned a dog, a large boxer. One day, the dog got loose and attacked one of the sheep. The bites got infected, gangrene developed, and the sheep died. Her partner, overcome with loneliness, took off for parts unknown. Well, not really unknown. A family on the other side of town owned a flock of sheep. Our sheep must have sensed their existence and decided to join them. Having been informed of this, Renato and David drove across town and brought her home. A few days later, the sheep repeated this excursion. Renato and David again went to retrieve her. This time they encountered not only the sheep but also another of that other family's animals . . . a full-grown bull . . . called Ferdinand. As they entered the yard, the bull noticed them and began to trot towards them. Lacking a red cape or anything else to distract the bull, Renato and David hightailed it up a nearby tree and stayed there until the bull could be corralled. The sheep was then granted permission to stay with her newfound friends. And Renato resigned himself to having to mow the entire lawn himself. Lesson learned.

CHAPTER 10

Christmas Eve Traditions

LYDIA LOVED ENTERTAINING, and nobody loved a party more than Renato. Now that they had the space, they indulged themselves. Lydia was in charge of the guest list and the food; Renato was in charge of the drinks. The days before Christmas Eve were hectic. There were last minute presents to be bought (Lydia), the Christmas tree to be set up (Renato) and decorated (me, Florence, David), and *crostoli* to be made. Crostoli are an Italian pastry of very thin rolled dough, fried and then sprinkled with a mixture of confectioners' and granulated sugar. Making them consumed an entire day and required a team of at least three who represented what I call the "Hierarchy of the Crostoli."

Number One in the hierarchy was Lydia, the Master Chef and chief arbiter of how things proceeded. She prepared the dough, which consisted of melted butter, flour, eggs, sugar, cinnamon, nutmeg, vanilla, lemon rind, lemon extract, 3 oz. rum, and 3 oz. grappa. After it had rested, she rolled it out paper-thin. For this she used a very large pastry board and an extra-long rolling pin. (I inherited these. When they needed to be replaced, I was unable to find either board or pin the right size, not at retail stores or wholesale outlets or at any baking utensil manufacturer. I was lucky to find two expert woodworkers. One, Harry Moore, a friend of my brother Bill, made me a pastry board 27" × 41" with a lip to keep it from sliding. The other, Les Wetherel of Sleeping Bear Woodworks, I discovered at the Morristown Crafts Fair. We discussed the choice of wood and settled on curly maple. I now have a 28" long × 1-5/8" diameter designer rolling pin signed by the artisan.)

Number Two in the hierarchy was the fryer. Frying was an important part of making crostoli. The dough had to be fried to just the right color—a pale golden tan. This required keeping the frying fat at just the right temperature. No thermometer was used, so the fryer needed to be sensitive to temperature changes in the fat. And the fat needed to be clean, which meant it had to be changed at least once during the cooking.

Number Three—the lowest rung, and usually one of the younger members of the team—was charged with sprinkling the crostoli with sugar after they were removed from the fat and set to drain on a layer of paper towels laid over three or four layers of newspaper. This had to be done judiciously . . . not too heavy and not too light . . . and once the crostoli had been sugared on one side, they needed to be gently turned over and sugared on the other side. This was the rung where I started out when I was 10 or 11.

After twenty years or so, I was allowed to try my hand at frying. But I was never officially promoted to rung Number Two. The sisterhood of the crostoli was resistant to newcomers. Though rung Number Three did have one great perk. Sampling a crostolo before the job was done was strictly forbidden. However, if one of the crostoli should, because of its fragility, happen to break, the sugarer could pop the pieces into her mouth and not be reprimanded.

After they were cooled and sugared, the crostoli were gently placed in layers separated by waxed paper, then the layers were put in large cardboard boxes to be stored in a cool dry place. They were Lydia's *pièce de résistance* at holiday gatherings.

Christmas Eve saw Renato's three living brothers (John had passed away in 1928 and Cesare in 1939) and their wives at the house for polenta (Renato's contribution cooked on the raised hearth in the family room) and *baccalà*—a traditional Venetian dish of dried salted codfish. The native Italians loved the baccalà, but the younger generation hated it. It was cut into bite-size pieces dressed with olive oil, garlic, and onion and served at room temperature. But it was tough. At that time, the Roman Catholic Church prescribed meatless meals on the eve of holy days. Lydia always made shrimp for those of us not enamored of baccalà. Forty years later in Mira, Italy, I discovered Baccalà Mantecato and fell in love with it. That version of baccalà is simmered in water and milk until tender and then beaten with olive oil, garlic, and heavy cream. Now I make polenta and baccalà every Christmas Eve.

On the Sunday between Christmas and New Year's Eve, Lydia often invited Renato's nieces and nephews for a celebration. There were twelve of them, and by the mid-1950s, all but two of them were married with children. Florence and Bill were both married—Florence to Joe Fiori in 1953, and Bill to Gloria Wright in 1954. This made for quite a group when added to Renato, Lydia, David, and me. Cocktails and hors d'oeuvres were the first order of business. Renato's cocktail of choice was a Manhattan and, other than a whiskey sour, was the only cocktail he knew how to make. So it became the customary cocktail accompanied by shrimp with a sauce that included enough horseradish to bring tears to your eyes and clear out your sinuses. Dinner was often filet mignon procured by Bill

VanderCloster, husband of niece Gilda, daughter of Renato's brother John, who worked part time for a caterer. Potatoes, vegetables, and salad varied. While Lydia was an accomplished cook, she was not known for her desserts. So these varied also.

After dessert and coffee there were crostoli with a glass of Asti Spumante. Prosecco was not yet well known in the U.S.

During all this eating, a goodly amount of red wine was drunk, and there was lots of conversation, gentle kidding, and laughter. We cousins always had a good time together and have continued to do so through the years. Opinions could be divergent and discussions could become very heated, but I don't remember anyone ever holding a grudge. We learned this behavior at our fathers' knees, so to speak. Discussions among the Belli brothers, often about the pinochle game they were playing, could degenerate into shouting matches with fists pounded on the table when laying down a card. I also remember a heated discussion one Christmas Eve regarding the year Uncle Arthur came to America. Was it 1922 or 1923? I was cowering in the wing chair in the living room, afraid it would come to blows, but it never did. I was also wondering why they were having this discussion at all since Uncle Arthur was part of it. Did his brothers think he couldn't remember what year he came? As the youngest of the brothers, Arthur was often treated like the baby and not given much credit. And did it matter whether he came in 1922 or 1923? It did to the Bellis, who aspired to be as precise with facts as they were when measuring lumber for their carpentry jobs. Just for the record, Ellis Island archives show Arthur Belli first entered the U.S. in 1923.

Chapter 11

Trip to Italy, 1953

1953 WAS A BIG YEAR for Lydia and Renato Belli and family of Saddle River. On July 4th, my older sister, Florence, married Joe Fiori of Clifton. I was a junior bridesmaid in the wedding party, which also included the maid of honor, Charlotte Hoitsma, and cousin Norma Marmoci and Gladys Schlanger as bridesmaids. The ceremony was at St. Gabriel's RC church in Saddle River. A reception for one hundred guests followed at the house on Chestnut Ridge Road. This event was what occasioned Lydia's desire for a canopy over the patio off the dining room of our house. She worried that either it would rain or be so hot that the patio would be useless for congregating without some protection. At this time, the only way to construct a canopy was to erect a series of metal pipes over which canvas was spread. Renato's response to this request was expected: "You want to spend how much?! To do what?! What are you, crazy?!" He also objected that the pipes would remain after the canvas was removed and ruin the look of the patio. I thought he was right about the look, but at 11 years old, I kept my mouth shut.

The canopy never materialized. July 4th was a beautiful, sunny day with very comfortable temperatures. Mother Nature managed to make both partners happy.

A couple of days before the wedding, Giuseppina appeared quite unexpectedly at the back door of our house. She had come from the farm in Gillette to offer her help with preparations. The trip involved someone driving her to the train station in Summit, then a long train ride from Summit to Ridgewood, and then a taxi from Ridgewood to Saddle River. Giuseppina was then 79 and the temperature was in the 90s. A feisty old lady was our Nonna.

Less than three weeks later, on July 23, Mom, Dad, David (age 9), and I (age 11), set sail for Italy on the American SS *Independence*. Dad hadn't been back to Italy for thirty-nine years due to WWI and WWII. Still an Italian citizen during WWI, he was considered a deserter because he didn't return to Italy to enlist and would have been arrested if he had returned afterwards. Then came the Great Depression and WWII. So this was a long awaited event for him. He still had one brother, Albino, and a sister, Alba, a nun, in Italy. Dad wrote to Albino about our arrival but received no reply. Transatlantic phone calls were difficult to arrange, and I doubt Dad had a phone number.

The SS *Independence* was the sister ship of the SS *Constitution*, which brought Grace Kelly to Monaco a few years later. We were all good sailors and thoroughly enjoyed ourselves onboard. Dad had purchased a 16mm movie camera a few months before and spent most of his time filming . . . seven rolls of film of just the blue ocean water. Mom enjoyed being served bouillon at 11:00 a.m. and tea at 4:00 p.m. in her deck chair. Dave and I explored the ship and spent a lot of time in the outdoor swimming pool.

When we arrived in Genoa, Dad sent a telegram to *zio* (Uncle) Albino to announce us. The next day he hired a car and driver to drive us to San Vito. The drive up was beautiful by way of Lago di Garda. I remember especially the century plants, which presumably live for one hundred years. Actually, they live for only twenty to thirty years, blossom only once, and then they die. I spent an hour or so gazing out the car window to spot a flowering one, but wasn't rewarded. I also remember that my silk scarf flew out the back window of the car but nobody was going to ask the driver to stop and retrieve it.

We arrived in the evening at Renato's brother Albino's house right on the main road in Resinego (a neighborhood of San Vito). He had not received the letter or the telegram. Didn't matter. We were welcomed with open arms. Everyone came out of the house to greet us. We then walked (thirty-nine paces) up the street to Hotel Dolomiti for dinner. We spent the night and most of the nights of the next four months in zio Albino's house. Only a handful of hotels were located in San Vito at that time, and all of them were full, as August is the most popular summer month for vacationing in Italy. And then all the hotels closed at the beginning of September.

Zio's house is still standing and must be well over 100 years old now. It has three floors with an eat-in kitchen and living room and wide entry hall on the first floor, three bedrooms and a bathroom on the second floor, and three more bedrooms and a bath on the third floor. Albino had a wife, Marina, and eight children: seven with his first wife, Domenica, who died in 1939; none with his second wife, Giuseppina; and a daughter with Marina. The eldest, Aldo, 30, was a priest at this point. The next in line, Lino, 29, was in medical school. Then Guido, 28, was married and the owner of a lumber business in San Vito. Tiziano, 25, ran the Hotel Pelmo, in the center of town, which Albino had built after WWII. Maria, 21, had studied hotel management and helped out at the hotel. Gianni, 19, and Giulio, 16, were both in college. And, finally, there was Nica, 5. Tiziano, Maria, Gianni, Giulio, and Nica all lived at home. Neither Albino nor Marina—or any of the children—spoke any English. David and I spoke no Italian. Dad and Mom were busy conversing in Italian and had no time to translate for us. I felt totally lost and insignificant.

San Vito di Cadore is 3,300' above sea level. My ears ached from the change in altitude. The house had no central heating, no refrigerator, a wood burning stove, and low-wattage electric bulbs. Commercial toilet paper was unheard of. We used old newspapers and bank statements. My first night there I shared a room with Maria. I wanted nothing more than to be back home in my own bed and with our cocker spaniel, Jeffrey, who was being looked after by my sister Florence and her husband. I cried for a week.

Our trunks arrived within a few days. Because we had come by ship, we didn't have to be concerned about baggage. So Mom packed two trunks plus a suitcase for each of us. I retain an image of her kneeling on the floor of the family room in our house in Saddle River to pack a trunk, probably only days after Florence's wedding. A surprise for David and me when we opened the trunk in Italy was a big bag of pink bubble gum shaped like cigars, compliments of my godmother, Tina Perini. She knew we wouldn't find any in Italy.

Zio Albino and his family opened their hearts and their home to us, and we stayed with them for several weeks. Zio and Marina gave up their bedroom to Mom and Dad, and I continued to share space with Maria. This allowed me to be privy to the fact that Gianni and Giulio, Maria's younger brothers, liked to play tricks on her. One night they short-sheeted her bed. The next morning Maria went about her business as if nothing had happened. She wasn't going to give them the satisfaction of having tricked her. I didn't understand that then, but now I do and like her for it.

For David and me, however, Gianni and Giulio were heaven-sent. They tried using the few English words they knew with us. This only made us laugh because their pronunciation was so bad. Empire State Building came out as *Em-pee-reh Stah-te Bwil-ding*. They taught us card games and joked with us. In short, they made us feel comfortable in what was for us a very foreign environment.

San Vito and all of Italy at that time were still recovering from WWII. They were on the cusp of what in a few years would be a huge economic boom based on tourism and manufacturing. But in 1953, most of that was yet to come. San Vito had a population of about 1,500. Most people didn't have a car or a telephone. Many kept a cow, chickens, and a horse. Stables were incorporated into homes. There was (and still is) only one main road. The national train line only extended to Calalzo (about 15 miles from San Vito). When you arrived there, you needed to switch to a narrow gauge railroad. The cars on this railroad were sky blue and white and looked more like a trolley than a train. There were three classes of cars. First class cars had compartments and overstuffed upholstered seats. I never saw anyone in these. Second class cars had less plush seats. Third class cars had no compartments and bare wooden benches. The trains ran on electric power, which could disappear at any given moment and cause delays.

Playing with Gianni and Giulio required David and me to learn some Italian, but Mom and Dad decided to also hire a tutor for us. The tutor turned out to be Mario Andreotta, an accountant who kept the books for several large hotels in nearby Cortina d'Ampezzo, site of the 1956 Winter Olympics. At that time, he was courting cousin Maria. His English was pretty good so he could explain things to our understanding. I don't remember anything in particular that we learned, but little by little we were beginning to speak Italian. Did anyone make note of the fact that being young and totally immersed is the best way to learn a new language? I don't think so. At this point Mom and Dad, who had never spoken Italian to their children, had decided it was time for David and me to learn. They, of course, continued to use English with us.

Mario Andreotta was quite a character. He stood about 5'3" tall and was a prime example of perpetual motion. Always on the go, he traveled on his Vespa motor scooter, the ubiquitous Italian mode of transportation in 1953. Not just his body but also his brain was always in motion, just like "Casey" (from a popular song) who waltzed with the "Strawberry Blonde" (that would be my song for him and Maria). At times it caused him to be forgetful, and once he even forgot his own children. He was living in Cortina with Maria and their two sons. He went from Cortina to Borca (about 9 miles), and after passing through San Vito, he dropped off his children with his parents. He traveled back to San Vito where he had business to conduct, and then he returned to Cortina. Maria asked, "Where are the kids?" OOPS! He might have been small in stature, but he had a heart of giant proportions, always willing to help anyone. In winter 1963 he found a job for me as an extra in the movie *The Pink Panther* filming in Cortina. (And several months later, he found me a permanent job as a teacher.) I will always remember him with a smile and great affection.

San Vito was, and still is, a very small town. This had its benefits for David and me. We could go out on our own and not get lost. We were completely safe. San Vito was devoid of crime. Most people either didn't lock their doors or left a key under the front doormat. We were free to roam. And we weren't the only Americans in San Vito that summer. During the late nineteenth and early twentieth centuries, many families had emigrated from San Vito to the U.S. (as in Belli family history). They often traveled back to visit relatives. That summer, a family named Fiori was there. It included a boy David's age and a girl my age. They were staying at the other end of town, and we became playmates. The family was from Ridgewood, N.J., a neighboring town of Saddle River.

Mr. Fiori owned the Ridgewood Taxi Company. Could they have been related to the Joe Fiori who had just married our sister, Florence? I don't remember. (In a strange coincidence years later [September 2016], while I was walking down the main street of San Vito, a local hotel owner waved to me and invited me in. He wanted to introduce me to one of his guests with the same name as my married one, Fiori. I sat down to talk to her. Of course we talked about our families. She told me her father or grandfather had been born in San Vito, and that she had been visiting since she was a little girl. Was there a chance her father owned Ridgewood Taxi Company? YES! And she had been my playmate of sixty-three years earlier!)

In 1953 in San Vito, most people, including zio Albino, didn't have a car. After several weeks, Dad decided to buy one. I don't know if he had planned on doing this before we'd left the States, but I doubt it, because neither Dad nor Mom had obtained an international driver's license. As an 11 year old, this problem never crossed my mind. Neither did I think about how Dad was going to pay for this car. Had he brought that much money with him? Did he borrow from his brother? If Albino had enough money to lend to him, why didn't Albino have a car himself? Whatever the case, one day Mom and Dad went to the provincial capital of Belluno and immediately obtained Italian driver's licenses. They also bought a FIAT 1500, a 4-door sedan. This was probably the biggest car in San Vito at the time, but it was small compared to American cars, and it received admiring inspection when they returned from Belluno. Back home Mom had her own car, but she never sat behind the wheel in Italy, France, or Switzerland, even though she was a better driver than Dad.

MILAN

Around the beginning of September we started off on our version of the Grand Tour. I have no idea who developed our itinerary, which included Italy, France, and Switzerland. Mom probably read about some places, and Dad most likely wanted to see Switzerland for its mountains and for the fact that his father had traveled there to build bridges.

Our first stop, though, was Milan. I have no memory of where we stayed or what attractions we visited. I don't think we ever made a hotel reservation in advance, not even in Paris or Rome. We just drove into town and started looking. Mom had an eye for upscale hotels, and, fortunately, Dad could afford them. Did we visit the Duomo and the Galleria Vittorio Emmanuele? We must have, as they are hard to miss. We did attend a performance at La Scala Opera House, the ballet *Les Sylphides*, because the opera season had not yet begun. Did we eat at "da Giannino," a restaurant much touted by Mom's friend and my godmother, Tina Perini? I doubt it. It was on the outskirts of the city, and Dad was not one for fancy restaurants. Did we window shop on the very, very chic Via Montenapoleone? Mom would have liked that. My most vivid memory is of visiting cousin Lino and his wife, Bepi. As we entered their apartment she was sitting in the kitchen, beating eggs and oil by hand to make mayonnaise. I was struck. Who knew mayonnaise didn't only come in jars?

COMO

From Milan we traveled north to Lake Como; on the way, we stopped to visit a man who had immigrated to America and then returned to Italy. I wish I could remember his name. He lived in Varese. I liked him. He must have asked me about myself; after I said I played the piano, he gifted me with one of his books that contained the plots of many operas. I devoured it.

I doubt we spent more than a night in Como. When traveling, Dad always wanted to get on to the next stop . . . or go home. And home in Europe always meant San Vito.

GLETSCH

Then it was through the Simplon Pass and into Switzerland. Our first night we stopped in the very small mountain town of Gletsch. We arrived at a hotel on the main road and went in: it was the Grand Hotel Glacier du Rhone. I think it's still there. It was our first encounter with Swiss hospitality, and I was enthralled. The public rooms were all paneled in dark wood. There was a fire burning in the fireplace. All was very warm and romantic. We had a delicious dinner and then retired to our rooms. David and I had a large room with bath. The twin beds had down quilts and TWO pillows on each. To me this was the height of luxury. So I luxuriated.

ADELBODEN

The next morning after a filling breakfast, we were off to Bern by way of Adelboden, a very small town about 40 miles off the main highway at the end of the road. It is the home of the International Girl Scout Chalet. I was a Girl Scout with little interest in seeing it, though I think Mom thought I should.

BERN

Then it was on to Bern, which I don't remember at all. I doubt we spent more than one night there, given Dad's propensity for moving on. I think he was more interested in visiting people, and we didn't know anyone in Bern. Mom, on the other hand, was all for seeing the sights. There were not a lot of sights to see in Bern in 1953.

PARIS

The next leg of our trip was Bern to Paris, France, 375 miles. We arrived in Paris, a city whose streets we didn't know, in the evening. We had no hotel reservation, and none of us spoke a word of French. That's not quite right. Mom may have taken an adult school course in French, but she couldn't put a complete sentence together.

It was now dark. My memory is that somehow we found a man who could speak a few words of Italian. He volunteered to take us to a suitable hotel. Dad said, "Hop in!". . . to a complete stranger! Mom, David, and I were sitting in the back seat, and this man was up front with Dad. I was trying hard to trust in my parents' judgment, but I was not at all comfortable with this man in the car. Mom was not showing her anxiety, if she had any. David was as quiet as a mouse. The man started to direct Dad to the hotel. He (the man) kept saying "A gauche! A gauche!" meaning "Left! Left!" Dad, of course, didn't understand until the man actually pointed. And we had learned our first French phrase.

We arrived at a hotel outside the center of the city. Mom insisted on seeing the room before checking in. It was definitely not up to her standards and seemed sleazy to me. So we took off on our own to find a hotel.

I don't remember how long we drove or if we asked any other strangers for advice, but we finally arrived in the center of Paris on the Champs-Élysées near the Arc de Triomphe. This area was more to Mom's liking. What's not to like about the ritziest part of Paris? We found lodging at the Georges Cinq about a block from the Arc. And by lodging, I mean a suite. Mom and Dad had their own bedroom, and David and I had separate rooms. The bathroom was huge. When the maid came with extra towels, Mom used the French she knew and told her to "... put it in the *bain* (bathroom), which (I realized when I later studied French) she mispronounced as *bine*. But Mom was praised for using her French, and the rest of us had learned our second French almost phrase. We delighted in repeating it. I can still hear us laughing.

We stayed five nights in Paris. Mom must have prevailed upon Dad, though it must have been tough for him to stay so long in one place that wasn't San Vito di Cadore or home. I'm sure we visited the Louvre, the Eiffel Tower, Notre Dame, and Versailles, but my memories are hazy. We were probably on tours with an English-speaking guide. I do remember the Mona Lisa and being surprised that it's painted on wood. We didn't visit any attractions that were especially for children, but Dave and I dutifully, and sometimes unwillingly, accompanied Mom and Dad to all the sights. True to our Italian roots, none of us was impressed by French cuisine, though Mom did develop a passion for *marrons glacés*—candied chestnuts. Neither did we visit Dior, Chanel, Balenciaga, or Cartier. Mom might have been intimidated by the language barrier. And the French, in their inimitable way back then, were not prone to trying to surmount it. Besides, I can just hear Dad saying, "You want to spend how much?! To buy what?! What are you, crazy?!"

Whatever else happened Paris did not work any magic on me. Though I have returned a couple of times, it's not one of my favorite cities.

LYON

From Paris we drove to Lyon and stayed just one night. Lyon was a big lace-making center, but I don't remember shopping for any.

TORINO

Our next stop was Torino, slightly south and east of Lyon. Why did we bypass Monaco and the French Riviera? I will never know. Perhaps not being able to speak French was becoming tiresome. Italian was our language.

I remember very little of Torino, except that it was the home of Lenci dolls, and Mom was looking to buy one. Lenci dolls were created in 1919 and were made entirely of wool felt. Their faces were hand painted; their eyes did not look straight at you but down and to the side giving them a suspicious or anxious expression. By 1953, they had become collectors' items. Mom had a hard time finding one, so she was unable to satisfy her desire. (Too bad, as they are now worth hundreds of dollars.) She did buy me a winter coat. I hated it. It was quite boxy, with a mandarin collar, and came to about mid-thigh. It was more like a jacket than a coat. It was black wool with large squares (maybe 8" square) that were defined by various color yarns—red, yellow, green. It may have been very much in style at the time, but I was uninterested. I never liked wearing it. I remember Torino as rainy and dark and possessed of many porticoed streets.

Many years later, I remarked to one of my Italian cousins that I regretted not seeing much of Torino and that I was thinking of returning to visit. He replied, "You didn't miss much." So I have yet to return.

CHIAVARI

From Torino we traveled south, completely avoiding the French Riviera. No more struggling with that language. We visited Portofino. Dad filmed David and me driving traps (small carriages) pulled by little ponies. From there it was on to Chiavari, a good-sized seaside town south of Genoa and east of Portofino. Our intent was to visit a couple of American expats, Mario and Linda Cerrutti, friends of Mom and Dad's friend, Tina Perini.

Mario and Linda made quite a pair. Both must have been in their sixties or seventies (at age 11, it's hard to determine, as everyone over 30 seems old). They had been enjoying the good life in Italy since they had sold their restaurant in Salt Lake City, Utah. Linda was short and plump with a mass of jet-black curls. Her preferred attire was a muumuu. Mario was white haired, and his well-developed paunch revealed how much he loved food. They had their own home in Chiavari. The garden included a grapefruit tree, which I found to be rather exotic. No one I knew in New Jersey or San Vito had one. But then, I was totally unfamiliar with the Mediterranean climate. We had dinner with the Cerruttis, but I don't remember the menu.

FRAMURA

From Chiavari we drove south along the coast to a very small town called Framura. Framura was the hometown of a longtime acquaintance of Dad's, Mario Barilari. Mario was the owner of Mario's Restaurant and Pizzeria on Van Houten Avenue in Clifton, N.J. The building was small when it opened, but the pizza was terrific and the business took off. When Mario's needed an extension, it was Dad who'd built it. At that time, Catholics still didn't eat meat on Fridays, so Friday night for pizza at Mario's was a regular occurrence in our family. When Mario passed away his children sold the business, and the quality of the pizza deteriorated. They are once again the owners, and the pizza is back to its deliciousness. The reason for our visit to Framura was to bring news of Mario to his relatives and possibly to bring them money. At that time, it was common for Italians in the U.S. to ask someone traveling to Italy to bring even small amounts of money to relatives in

Italy. (I, myself, was asked that when I traveled there in 1962.) I guess they didn't trust the U.S. (or, more likely, the Italian) postal service.

Framura is a medieval village that is part of the Cinque Terre, which at that time was not the chic location to visit that it is today. Most of the towns in the area are inaccessible by car, and Framura is one of them. Mom and Dad left David and me in the car parked on the side of the road and proceeded to descend the steep path down to the seaside village. It was a sunny, hot day; we became easily bored. The only thing left to do was quarrel.

PARMA and BIBBIANO

From Framura we went east and inland to Parma. I remember stopping for lunch. Dad bought a huge chunk of Parmigiano Reggiano cheese and a couple of loaves of bread. I was hooked on the cheese from then on. I have no idea what it cost then, but now it's rather pricey. Instead, I use less expensive Grana Padano. This is the same recipe but made with the milk of cows from the Po valley instead of cows from Reggio Emilia.

From Parma we continued on to a very small town called Bibbiano. Dad's sister, Alba, who was a nun, had lived in the convent here since she had been a young woman. We visited her there. I remember our waiting for Sister Alba to join us in the main room. At this point she was 61 years old and most likely hadn't seen Dad for over forty years. I understood nothing of their conversation (my Italian was still meager) and nobody was translating. But I think this visit was a loving gesture on Dad's part. He held a grudge against the Catholic Church because Sister Alba had not been allowed to leave the convent to visit her parents when they were dying. I don't remember any of my relatives in Italy ever visiting her.

Bibbiano is important in the history of Parmigiano Reggiano cheese. The monks in the Benedictine monastery discovered the "recipe" for it: good quality milk (that of the evening and the morning), fire (two heatings), rennet (a type of curdled milk for coagulation), and salt. The mixture left to mature for a whole year. In 1145, the abbot of the monastery coined the term *formadio*, that is, "God's wheel of cheese," to honor its excellence. It's also a play on words since *formaggio* is the Italian word for cheese. This occasioned an epochal change in the agriculture of the town, which had, until then, been limited to sheep's milk cheese. For hundreds of years, farmers in the area rented land from the monastery in exchange for money, goods (sheep), and cheese. Most historians agree that the birthplace of good quality Parmigiano Reggiano in large quantities was Bibbiano in the 1700s (per Wikipedia).

We stayed the night at an inn in Bibbiano. David and I had rooms separate from Mom and Dad, but none of the rooms had a bathroom or even just a sink. The next morning the maid brought us a large bowl and a big pitcher of water. Was there a toilet down the hall? Did I have a chamber pot? I don't remember. I do remember Dad telling David young men used to shun the chamber pot and piss right out the window! He wasn't recommending Dave do the same. To me—who was used to the all the modern conveniences of our home in Saddle River—this all seemed rather primitive, and yet intriguing.

MONTECATINI TERME

The next day, it was on to Montecatini Terme. Montecatini is a spa town in northern Tuscany. Its mud baths were known as far back as Roman times, but the town reached its height of popularity during the early years of the twentieth century, the *Belle Epoque* years between the late nineteenth century and World War I. Verdi, Puccini, Leoncavallo, and even King

Vittorio Emanuele II came to enjoy the mud baths and drink the waters. Mom wanted to drink the curative waters. I don't know if she was trying to alleviate a particular ailment or just wanted to do the thing to do in Montecatini. Though there were no mud baths for any of us, we all tried the waters. I don't remember anyone else's reaction, but I took one sip and had enough. They were very warm, very salty, and smelled of rotten eggs from the sulphur content. I doubt that Mom spent more than one day at this activity.

We stayed at the Hotel Moderno where Dave and I were "adopted" by the two waiters in the dining room. They probably spoke some English, and we were learning a bit more Italian. They made our stay in Montecatini much more enjoyable, and I still have a picture of them with Dave in front of the hotel. Montecatini is about a half hour by car, between Florence and Pisa. So we made day trips to both these places.

Pisa can be seen in a day. Of course, the most famous monument is the leaning tower. David and I climbed to the top on the narrow, spiraling stairway. After this excitement, the Baptistry and Duomo in the same square paled in comparison.

Florence is so full of things to see that I'm sure we must have spent more than one day there, but I remember little. I do remember Michelangelo's David. What young girl wouldn't? (Remember, I was 11.) Years later when I visited Florence with my daughters, Lydia (who was 11) entered the hall where the David stands, took one look, and gasped. And to think Michelangelo was in his early twenties when he sculpted this.

I had my own camera and took pictures of what interested me . . . the Ponte Vecchio, the doors on the Duomo and baptistery, a couple of panoramic shots from Piazzale Michelangelo on the other side of the Arno from historic Florence. I also have one shot of a bombed out building near the river. In 1953, Florence was still recovering from WWII.

For me the ruins held little connection, just another sight to photograph. The continental U.S. hadn't experienced any of the war, and by 1953, most Americans had put it far behind them.

ROME

Our travels took us next to Rome. On the way we visited the American and British military cemeteries in Anzio. One of our relatives who survived the war debarked there with other American troops. As usual, we had made no advance reservations, but this time at least Dad and Mom spoke the language. And Mom's eye for upscale hotels led us to the Hotel Massimo d'Azeglio. Either that or someone in San Vito had recommended it. This was a four-star hotel, a stone's throw from the main train station. It is still in business today.

We must have stayed a week in Rome, during which time we took guided tours. What interested me, as attested to by my photos, were the Roman Forum, the Colosseum, the Monument to Vittorio Emanuele II, St. Peter's Basilica, Castel Sant'Angelo, and the Arch of Constantine. Also, the train station. It was quite new and of a strikingly modern design. To this day, its basic structure hasn't changed and is still impressive. And to this day, history and architecture still give me pleasure.

The Pope (Pius XII) was not in residence in Rome at that time of year, so we journeyed to Castel Gandolfo, his summer residence. I don't remember seeing him, but I did snap a picture of the Swiss Guard.

When we didn't take a tour bus, Dad drove us around Rome. Traffic in Rome, even in 1953, was chaotic. At one intersection Dad made an illegal turn and was stopped by a traffic cop. (In general, Mom was impressed by their uniforms and the balletic way in which they moved their arms to direct traffic.) Dad tried to explain that he was an American and not familiar with Roman traffic laws. The cop wasn't having any of it. He responded, "You're driving an Italian car, you have an Italian driver's license, and you speak perfect Italian. Don't tell me you don't know the law. Pay me the fine right now." And Dad paid him right there.

NAPLES

From Rome we drove farther south to Naples. Naples . . . the home of the pizza. Dave and I loved pizza. In Italy, pizza is usually made as an individual dish. At our first lunch in Naples, Dave and I both ordered one. Our mouths were watering. To our great disappointment, the pizza arrived drowning in olive oil. Not what we were used to. The recipe must have lost something in translation when it crossed the ocean.

As a city, Naples did not appeal to me. It was too hot and too chaotic and too dirty. The only thing I remember of the city itself is eating dinner at a restaurant with tables outside. A woman at one of the nearby tables had a huge beetle on her shin. She was either unaware of it or ignoring it. Either way, I thought it weird. At the same restaurant, a singer was strolling around the tables, entertaining. Dad gave him a tip (I don't remember how much), which the singer threw back at him indicating it was too little. Dad shrugged. From Naples we took a day trip to Pompeii. This I found fascinating and happily returned there in 1962.

AMALFI COAST

From Naples it was a short drive south to Sorrento. We must have spent the night there and taken the ferry to Capri the next day. I fell in love with Capri. It was the perfect time of year to be there, and it wasn't yet victim to hordes of tourists as it is today. Then we drove east along the coast to Amalfi. It was a beautiful, scenic drive of which I remember nothing. I did snap a picture of the town of Amalfi. This was as far south as we went. From there we traveled north and east to Pescara on the Adriatic.

ADRIATIC COAST

We continued traveling north along the coast. Just southwest of Rimini and 10 miles inland is the landlocked Republic of San Marino, the fifth smallest country in the world. It covers just 24 square miles. Monte Titano, its 2,200 foot central land mass has three summits, each topped by a medieval fortress. Its romantic, fairy-tale look quite appealed to this 11 year old but not to the males with me. We stayed long enough to have our passports stamped and to send postcards with the San Marino postage stamp.

From here we must have gone on to Padova. I write this because I have a picture of David and me feeding the pigeons in front of the Basilica di Sant'Antonio, the patron saint of Padova. Dad is in the picture with us, so Mom must have taken it. Also in the picture is Signora Passacantando, a friend of Mom and Dad's. Her name enchanted me. Literally translated it means "passes while singing." They had another acquaintance named Fumagalli, which means "smokes roosters." Many Italian surnames developed, as English ones did, by being based on relationships (Johnson, Anderson), one's job (Carpenter, Taylor, Bishop), or even physical characteristics (Short). But Italian ones also seem much more creative.

Padova is a city known by the Romans. Its university is the second oldest in Italy after the one in Bologna and was founded in 1222 by students and professors who were leaving Bologna in search of more academic freedom. Galileo taught there in the sixteenth and seventeenth centuries. One can still visit the auditorium where he lectured.

Padova is only forty-five minutes by car from Venice. Now it seems logical to me to have gone there next, but I don't remember Venice at all. We may have gone at another time since I'm sure Mom would have wanted to see it, but Dad would have wanted to stay in San Vito. I do remember bringing home a little glass horse, a typical souvenir of Venice, so we must have visited at some point. Venice didn't capture my heart at this time. That would take a couple more trips. I'm not sure why. Maybe because I was too young to be allowed to wander off on my own and enjoy getting lost.

SAN VITO

I think we were all glad to get back to San Vito di Cadore. We had enjoyed our trip but had had enough of sightseeing, hotels, and riding in a car. I think Dave and I were especially glad because San Vito was a very safe environment and we were allowed the run of the town. By now it was early October. Our cousins Gianni and Giulio had not returned to school. They were studying at home as was possible in Italy. They would return to school only for exams. So we had company. And our Italian was getting better.

From San Vito we took short trips to visit relatives, not an activity of choice for a 12 (I had celebrated my 12th birthday on September 27) and a 10 year old. Zio Albino's oldest son, Aldo, was a priest in Visome about forty-five minutes away. All I remember of our visit there is that Visome seemed like a very poor town, and that high on a hill we picked hickory nuts, a favorite of mine. The respectful title for a priest in Italy is Don, so Aldo was always called Don Aldo even among the family. For a long time I thought his name was Donald.

CORDENONS

Born in Cordenons, Mom had only one cousin remaining there. We stayed in the house where Mom had been born. She and I shared a bed. I remember her telling me that her grandparents raised silkworms. Mom's sister, Anna, writes about this in her memoir:

> I remember going to the drugstore (farmacia) where she [grandma] bought a small bottle of silkworm eggs and several large blue paper blotters. That evening when we went to bed (I slept with her), she rolled down the blanket and sheets and placed the two blotters down the center of the mattress, spread the eggs on them, and covered them with the other two blotters. The idea in using blotters was to keep the tiny eggs from rolling off the blotters. Then she placed the sheets and blankets on as usual. She slept on one side and I on the other, leaving the center space for the blotters [that] would warm up sufficiently during the night to start the eggs hatching. She watched them closely, and as soon as she saw the slightest movement of the eggs she moved them to the kitchen and placed them on the benches near the fireplace. Then as the eggs hatched, she began to feed them young finely chopped mulberry leaves. Soon there was not enough room in the kitchen and they were moved to the attic where there were many trays with branches and leaves from the mulberry trees prepared by father. We had a field of mulberry trees for this purpose. Grandma watched the

> worms as they matured and finally formed cocoons, which she gathered and sold to the local silk factory (La Filanda). This was a yearly project.
>
> —From Anna DePiero's book, *Remembrances* (Turrin, 1989).

Cordenons sits on a large plain with mountains in the distance. The area has been part of the Roman, Venetian, Napoleonic, and Austro-Hungarian empires, but it didn't become an incorporated city until 1866, after the unification of Italy. Until the mid-twentieth century its main business was agriculture. Indeed, when Angelo DePiero was asked what his occupation was in order for it to be recorded in a ship's manifest, he answered "peasant."

The terrain is completely level. Bicycles materialized from somewhere, and David and I took full advantage. From being carted around to visit adults whom we could neither understand nor converse with, this was our FREEDOM! I still can see me enjoying it. One thing I didn't like, though. During one visit I asked to use the toilet and was directed to a hole in the ground, albeit enclosed, in the back yard. I was shocked, but what could I do? I made the best of it.

We also went as far as Trieste, a city I fell in love with later in life. For many years, it was a free port, and the sense of freedom there is palpable. Approaching by train, you get a marvelous view of the bay and the city. Its steep hills come right down to the water's edge. Our intent was, as was often the case, to visit relatives or friends of relatives. This time it was the family of Mom's sister, Anna. Anna had married a man named Anthony Turrin, and they owned a poultry farm in Gillette, New Jersey. Anthony's family also had a poultry business in Trieste. When we arrived in the evening, they were candling eggs. I had never seen or heard of this operation before and was fascinated.

Back in San Vito, Dad had convinced Albino that it was time for cousin Maria and Mario Andreotta to get married, and that it would be a good idea to have the ceremony while we were there. If I remember correctly the date was set for October 2, 1953, also the anniversary of Mom and Dad's wedding. Not a lot of time for preparation, but the women of the family worked furiously. Maria purchased a long white wedding gown. Maria is the fifth of seven children that Albino had with his first wife, Domenica, who passed away in 1939 as I mentioned earlier. He then married her sister, Giuseppina, who also died after a few years. For his third wife he took Marina and they had a daughter, Domenica (Nica), who at this time was age 5. Marina was a loving mother and stepmother who did her all for the whole family. She and Mom, along with a few neighbors, baked a mountain of little pastries for the wedding day. The ceremony was set for 11:00 a.m. Around 9:00 a.m., most of the wedding guests (about thirty) arrived at Albino's home and were served coffee and pastries. Around 10:30, we all—including the bride and groom—walked the almost a mile to the church in the center of town. No superstition about the groom seeing the bride before the wedding. The wedding party included the bride, groom, and two witnesses . . . no ushers or bridesmaids. At the church, the bride merely walked up the aisle with the best man, and the groom walked up with the maid of honor. Marina did not attend the ceremony but stayed home to clean up. There must have been a reception, but I don't remember it.

SAN VITO

We spent our remaining time in San Vito. Even then, San Vito was known as a summer and winter resort town. Its population swelled during July and August and from Christmas to March. But now it was October, and the hotels were all closed. David's and my teachers had not given us any work to do to keep up with our classes back home. They felt confident we could catch up when we returned. And they must have been right because I don't remember feeling behind with the material. So we were quite free to amuse ourselves as we saw fit.

I remember accompanying the farmhands, Piero and Luigi, with the horse and wagon to gather hay. We had fun jumping on the haystacks, but at one point I ended up with my head just behind the horse's hoof. Luigi gave me a good chewing out. If the horse had lifted its hoof, I would have been kicked in the head. After lunch, which the farmhands shared with all of us, we played cards with them. We used old-fashioned Italian cards with pictures and symbols with no relation to a modern deck of playing cards. I had a hard time keeping them straight. They're still made today, and I still am confused.

Mom found a way for me to occupy some of my time. The family next door had a daughter a few years older than I. She was into needlework. I had learned some stitches already. Mom asked the girl to transfer a pattern to a piece of heavy muslin for me to embroider. She did, and I learned thread count embroidery . . . two threads of the fabric for every outline stitch. The thread was red, and the muslin was unbleached. The piece was probably 14" × 14", so it kept me busy for a good while. When it was finished and we returned home, we put a back on it and made it into a pillow. It seems to me Mom commissioned the girl to make a matching one in green thread. I was proud of mine.

The *Dolomites* (mountains) around San Vito include Monte Marcora (10,348' high), Monte Antelao (10,705' high), and Monte Pelmo (10,394' high). Below the tree line they are covered with more than one species of pine and a few maples. In the fall, some of these pines turn golden. Mixed in with the evergreens they create a stunning panorama.

Slaughtering a Pig

Zio Albino had raised a pig. It lived imprisoned in a little shed behind zio's house. Every night, the maid would fix its dinner—a pail full of slop, leftovers from dinner. This pig ate like a gourmet. While we were in San Vito, it was time to slaughter the pig. This would provide food for guests at Albino's Hotel Pelmo and also for his immediate family. At that time there were itinerant handymen who traveled around and performed various jobs . . . knife sharpening, umbrella repairing, hay gathering. I don't know for sure if a few of these were who slaughtered the pig, but they very well might have been.

David and I did not see the actual slaughter. I think Mom and Dad deliberately managed to have us return from an outing a little after it took place. This was probably a good thing. From what I've since read, the pig would have put up an awful screaming and kicking fight when being dragged from its little shed. Not something that would induce sweet dreams. When David and I arrived in the back yard, the pig was already in a wooden trough filled with boiling water. The men were shaving it. Could the bristles have been useful for something else? Were they saved? I don't know. After the pig was completely shaved, the men strung the pig up on a bar suspended over the entrance to the barn. One of the men used a large knife to slit the pig down the middle from end to end. Blood and guts gushed out. The pig was hosed down, and then the man reached inside and removed the rest of the entrails. When the pig had dried off, it was taken up to the Hotel Pelmo where a butcher carved it up.

Like most of what I experienced in San Vito, this whole procedure was far removed from anything I'd ever witnessed back in Saddle River. I was fascinated and slightly disappointed that I hadn't seen the actual slaughter. Part of the story was missing.

Homeward Bound

We had now been in Italy for close to four months. David and I had missed almost three months of school. As I mentioned earlier, our teachers, when questioned before we left, had agreed that the absence would not affect our learning. And, indeed, it didn't. I don't remember having any difficulty catching up when we got back.

A task that Dad had while in San Vito was to settle up the estate of his parents. At that time, many Italians died intestate and left the division of property to their descendants. Dad and his brothers in the U.S. had previously decided that since zio Albino had been the one to stay in Italy, carry on the business, and take care of the parents until they died, they would leave any inheritance to him. However, Dad took it upon himself to convince Albino to return to the U.S. with us to reconnect with his other brothers.

We sailed from Genoa on the SS *Independence* towards the end of November. For some reason, Mom, Dad, and Albino, along with his wife and his son, Tiziano, traveled to Genoa a few days before the sailing (maybe Albino needed to present himself at the U.S. Consulate). David and I were left at the house in San Vito with the housekeeper and Albino's son Gianni, age 19. A couple of days later, we journeyed to Genoa with Gianni's brother, Guido, and his wife, Anna. Our train was scheduled to leave San Vito at 5:30 a.m. It was still dark and we were the only ones out. Gianni helped us carry our luggage to the station, every once in a while shouting "*Facchino*!!!!" (porter). David and I thought this was hilarious. Anna and Guido, not so much. The train from San Vito took us only as far as Calalzo (20 km) where Guido needed to leave the train to buy our tickets for the rest of the trip. I remember worrying that he wouldn't make it back to the train in time. Anna reassured me, and he did.

Anna, Guido, David, and I arrived in Genoa safe and sound. I don't remember lodging at a hotel, so maybe we boarded the ship immediately. I do remember zio Albino's family members coming aboard to say their last farewells AND EVERYONE CRYING PROFUSELY. When we had arrived in San Vito, I cried for a week. Now that we were leaving Italy, I cried again. I had met brand new relatives, and I felt really liked and accepted by them. I don't know if I could have verbalized this then. All I knew was that I hated to leave. And from then on a major goal in my life has always been how to get back to Italy.

Our journey back to New York was largely uneventful. I think we celebrated Thanksgiving onboard the ship. I do remember that one day at lunch I decided to try roast duck. I didn't like it and have never tried it again. The weather in November can be stormy, and we did have a couple of days of a very rocky boat. But we were all good sailors and managed to keep our meals down. Based on this experience at age 12, I believed that when I became pregnant I would not suffer from morning sickness. (Eleven years later I was to be proven excruciatingly wrong.)

After nine days, we arrived in New York City. Florence and her husband, Joe, met us at the dock. They brought us back to Saddle River where they had prepared a welcome home dinner complete with a banner that expressed how happy they were to have us back.

David and I started school immediately. On my first day in eighth grade a very strange thing happened. Our teacher, Frank Almroth, asked me about the trip and then asked me to say something in Italian. I said: "*Napoli e` sporca*" (Naples is dirty), and I didn't translate it. Sitting across from me was a boy who lived in what was considered "the other side of the tracks" in Saddle River. A member of the mysterious, multiracial Jackson Whites clan, he never attended school regularly. As soon as I said, in Italian, "Napoli e` sporca," he said in English, "So am I." Where did that come from? I was stunned. Could he somewhere have learned some Italian? Did what I said sound like some dialect he spoke? What did he think I said? No one asked. After he said it, he laughed. Was it a joke? Was he just nervous? It still puzzles me.

In no time, David and I were busy with schoolwork, Mom was wrapped up in preparations for Christmas, and Dad, whose construction business was slack in the winter, was helping Albino visit as many relatives and friends as possible.

Our Italian odyssey had come to an end.

Renato, Lydia, Lynn, and David aboard the SS Independence, *en route to Italy, July 1953.*

David with our friendly waiters in Montecatini, Italy.

CHAPTER 12

Life Cycles

THANKS TO RENATO'S HEROIC EFFORT, ties with his family were reconnected and have remained strong to this day. Following this epic trip, life went on apace at Belli Acres in Saddle River, N.J.

With the passing of years came medical episodes. In the late 1950s, Lydia was diagnosed with adult onset diabetes as her mother had been before and her sister Mary was shortly after. This limited her participation in the eating and drinking at parties, but she never stopped entertaining. Though she hated having to inject herself with insulin, she was scrupulous about doing it, just like Giuseppina had been. As she aged, Giuseppina would sometimes inject a bit too much. If we saw her sitting quietly and getting rather glassy eyed, we'd offer her a glass of orange juice or a lollipop, and things would right themselves. In the early 1960s, Lydia slipped on a patch of ice and broke her hip, which was repaired by a surgeon who inserted a pin. And I never knew her to complain about walking or standing.

On August 30, 1957, Giuseppina passed away. At the time, Lydia, David, and I were in Italy. It happened to be Labor Day weekend in the U.S., and a mass of American tourists were leaving Italy to begin school or work back home. There were no seats available on any flights to New York, so we were unable to attend the funeral, though Lydia had a Mass said in San Vito. Needless to say, we were deeply saddened.

In the fall of 1958, at a family dinner at a restaurant in upstate New York, Renato suffered a minor heart attack. Fortunately when it happened, he was sitting next to a physician, his nephew Lino, who was visiting from Italy. And the only doctor in town was a retired cardiologist who had a small care facility in his home. Renato spent a week in bed there and then returned to Saddle River. He remained as active as ever and never had another attack. He didn't particularly watch his diet, so could his longevity have been thanks to all the red wine?

Over the next twenty years, Bill, Lynn, and David all married.

And Lydia and Renato were gifted with four loving grandchildren. When David married Catherine Becht in 1973, Renato wore the tailor-made suit he had worn at his own wedding forty-seven years earlier. It fit him to a T.

On October 2, 1976, Lydia and Renato celebrated fifty years of marriage with a dinner dance hosted by their children and grandchildren at the Robin Hood Inn in Clifton. Lydia's two surviving siblings, Anna and Jack, attended, along with Renato's niece Maria Andreotta and her husband, Mario, from Italy, and eighty other nieces and nephews and good friends. In honor of the occasion, Renato's nephew Don Aldo Belli wrote and published a short history of the Belli Codan family in Italy and how they immigrated to America. A leather-bound copy was presented to Lydia and Renato at the dinner. This was the first effort at chronicling Belli family history. I translated the book into English, so it is now printed in both languages, making it accessible to family on both sides of the ocean.

Following is how Lydia remembered the day as she recorded it in a scrapbook for the occasion.

How We Celebrated Our Day

All of our children and grandchildren were with us:

- Florence Fiori
- William and wife, Gloria
- Lynn and husband, Romeo Fiori, and their daughters, Lydia June and Emily Denise
- R. David and wife, Catharine, and their son Jonathan

A family picture was taken at home at Belli Acres. We all attended a 5:00 p.m. Mass in Saint Gabriel's Church, Saddle River; and Msgr. David Price gave us the Apostolic Blessing. Mario and Maria (our neice [sic] and husband) arrived Oct. 1st from Cortina, Italy, to represent our families there.

At 6:30 p.m. we went to the Robin Hood Inn where our children had planned a festive celebration with nephews, nieces, other relatives and friends, about 85 people altogether, where liquid and solid refreshments flowed for the evening and there was much pleasant and lively conversation.

Jay's Orchestra provided delightful music for listening and dancing and all joined in the gaiety of the evening.

Moments to Remember

> The highlight of the evening was a musical production composed by Lynn and executed by our talented children. In prose and song they exposed to all the courtship and married life of Mom and Dad. It brought down the house and we loved it.
>
> Thank you all! Lynn in particular, who also put together a collage of pictures of 50 years of Belli family togetherness (very amusing). Altogether a labor of love and much appreciated.

I wrote this "operetta," and the performers were called the "B.B.B.F.F.W. Opera Company," i.e., Belli, Belli, Becht, Fiori, Fiori & Wright. The musical numbers were old popular songs to which I had written new lyrics. Luckily, the band we had hired knew all the songs and were able to accompany us. This greatly added to the professionalism of the performance and covered up any wrong notes hit by the performers. A boon to all.

Lydia and Renato's 40th wedding anniversary, October 2, 1966. From left: Mary DePiero Wunsch, Madeline Belli (wife of Luigi), Anna DePiero Turrin, Lucia Belli (wife of Arturo), Arturo Belli, Luigi Belli, Lydia, David Belli, Florence Belli Fiori, and Renato. Kneeling: Lynn Belli Fiori and Lydia Fiori.

Renato and Lydia, March 24, 1974.

Raking party Saddle River, 1975. Sitting: Gladys Schlanger, Lydia Fiori (daughter of Lynn Belli Fiori), and Gilda Belli VanderCloster. Standing: Florence Belli Fiori, David Belli, Renato, and Caspar Amoruso.

Lydia's 70th birthday, May 27, 1976.

Lydia and Renato's 50th wedding celebration, October 2, 1976.

Lydia, Renato, Anna DePiero Turrin (Lydia's sister and matron of honor), and Jack DePiero (Lydia and Anna's brother) at the 50th wedding celebration.

Giuseppina's 80th birthday in 1954. From left: Giuseppina, daughter Mary, granddaughter Dorothy Wunsch Maresca, and great-granddaughter Judy Maresca.

Less than a year after their 50th anniversary, Lydia and Renato sold the house in Saddle River and moved back to Clifton to a multi-level house at 2 Canterbury Court. By that time, they were both in their seventies, and the house and grounds in Saddle River had become too much for them to maintain on their own. Landscapers were not as popular then as they are now to look after one's property. And if one had been suggested, I'm sure Renato's response would have been, "You want to spend how much?!" etc., etc. He did, however, try inveigling his children, nephews and nieces, and any friends of theirs to help. Once a year, in the fall, we would be invited for dinner, but before we could break out the Manhattans and party we had to rake leaves from the 2 acres of grounds around the house.

On February 22, 1977 Renato celebrated his 80th birthday with a small gathering—again at the Robin Hood Inn. Celebrating with him was Lydia's brother, Jack, also born in

1897. Jack was retired from the U.S. Postal Service and living in Marathon, Florida. He drove himself up to New Jersey for the occasion with the same grit that had gotten Giuseppina to Saddle River to help with wedding preparations. And isn't it remarkable that Jack, born in Delaware, and Renato, born in Italy, not only became brothers-in-law but also celebrated this day together?

After a final trip to Italy in the summer of 1977, Lydia and Renato enjoyed their remaining years in their new home, with frequent visits from their children and grandchildren and even a few visits from the family in Italy. In September 1982, Lydia suffered a heart attack. When home from the hospital, she became overwhelmed by the turn her life had taken, and she retreated into her childhood. In late July 1985, she fell at home and reinjured her hip. Surgery corrected the hip, but she passed away of a heart attack in the hospital. Life had become too much for her.

All of his married life, Renato had declared that he had married a woman nine years younger than he was so that she would always be there to take care of him. Like the best laid plans of mice and men, this plan also went astray. Renato was now alone and needed to take care of himself. Fortunately, he had his sister-in-law, Lucia, widow of his brother Arthur, to help. And he learned how to use a stove and a washing machine. He didn't go out much, but we had a standing date once a week on Sunday to go out for dinner. When we met one Sunday in December 1986, Renato insisted he didn't want to go out; I insisted I didn't want to cook dinner. He disappeared into the kitchen, heated up leftovers, set the table, and called me when things were ready. If only Lydia could have seen it. Or better yet, if she could have been the recipient of a similar gesture. For she, like Renato, wanted to be taken care of, pampered. And pampering did not come easily to Renato.

The day after we dined on his delectable leftovers, Renato suffered a stroke, which left him with little use of his right side. Speech was difficult. After a few weeks in hospital, he was transferred to a nursing home. There was no talk of physical therapy, but his mind was sharp, and he was able to sit in a wheelchair.

On February 22, 1987, Renato celebrated his 90th birthday with family and ice cream. Five weeks later he stopped eating. When I reminded him of the consequences, he merely nodded. I didn't have the heart to argue with him. In Italy, a person's last days are called his *agonia* (agony), no matter what his condition. Renato's last week was truly spent in mental agony, complete with moaning and writhing. It must have been very difficult for him to leave. As if symbolic of that, for his last moments, the heavens provided a background of thunder, lightning and heavy rain.

During their final trip to San Vito in 1977, Renato and Lydia stayed in the house on the banks of the Boite River where Renato had grown up. At a family gathering of all his nephews and nieces, Renato had offered this reflection:

> Each night before going to bed I open the window and look at the rushing water of the Boite. I am touched because it is still the same river of my boyhood. Then, I close the window only to open it another time. Then, I close it again and get in bed. I listen to the sound of the ever rushing water and think that it will still be flowing when I return in a few years and when my children and grandchildren and great-grandchildren visit. It will always be the same and always be different like the life of the Codan family that always goes on and is always the same and is always different.

This brings me to the end of this history. I encourage my children, grandchildren and great-grandchildren to continue it. Start now. Ask questions, keep a diary, gather stories about your family. Don't wait until the only person with the answer isn't here anymore.

—LYNN BELLI FIORI
January 8, 2021

Map showing locations of San Vito and Cordenons, Italy.

Addenda

SAN VITO DI CADORE

San Vito di Cadore is a small town in northeastern Italy, 33 miles from the Austrian border. It sits at an altitude of 3,317'. among the Dolomite Mountains, a UNESCO World Heritage site. At the beginning of the twentieth century it numbered 2,000 inhabitants, but between 1901 and 1911 over 500 residents immigrated—mostly to the U.S. but also to Germany and other countries in Europe. Why? Because the land and climate could not produce enough to feed the population. Potatoes were the major crop. Meat was rarely eaten. Polenta was on the table every day. Baccalà was the only fish available because it could be stored. Fresh fruit was a dream unless someone became sick and an orange could be procured.

Today, San Vito thrives on tourism, skiing and mountain climbing.

BORCA DI CADORE

Borca is the next town south of San Vito of which it is half the size and has half the population. Given Borca's proximity to San Vito, it is quite possible that Giuseppina Varettoni knew of the Belli Family. The Bellis may even have patronized Bortolo Varettoni's shoe repair shop.

CORDENONS

In 1866, when Angelo DePiero was born, Cordenons had slightly less than 5,000 inhabitants. Today, it numbers 18,433. Previously it produced paper, silk, and cotton. Today, it is used as a bedroom community, and workers travel to adjacent cities such as Pordenone and Udine for their jobs.

RESEARCH

Since that day in 1926, much has been written and passed on orally about Renato's family but not so much about Lydia's. Her sister Anna's collections of *Remembrances* filled in some history, but I wanted to learn more. When did her father, Angelo, come to this country? What did he do for a living? How did he meet Giuseppina? Where were they married?

I started my search in Cordenons, Italy, where both Lydia and her father had been born. Cordenons is a small town in the province of Pordenone in northeastern Italy about halfway between Venice and Trieste. I hadn't been back there in fifty-seven years, and at that time Renato had driven us. This time, I went by train from Venice to Pordenone (one hour), and then by bus from Pordenone to Cordenons (20 mins.). Rather, it should have been 20 minutes, but after I purchased my ticket at the nearest bar, I waited for the bus at a stop where the sign listed Cordenons, among other stops. It never dawned on me that the stops were listed in the order that the bus passed through them, so with Cordenons at the top of the list, it meant the bus had already been there when it arrived where I was. The bus came. I got on. After the expected 20 minutes or so, I was the last remaining passenger. We were in a very residential area, and the bus driver pulled into a large parking lot. He stopped the bus and turned off the motor. "Is this Cordenons?" "No. Cordenons is at the other end of the route." So I sat and waited for 15 minutes, and then we were off to Cordenons.

Around 11:30 a.m. I arrived at the Ufficio Anagrafe (Hall of Records). Six people were ahead of me in line. I took a number from the ubiquitous number machine. Someone ahead of me decided to leave and left his ticket on the machine. A man who hadn't been there before walked in, took the ticket and walked up to a window ahead of all the rest of us! A typical Italian ploy I learned about through bitter experience.

Angelo was born in 1866. When I finally spoke with someone, I learned that this office only had records as far back as 1871. I was sent to the rectory of the Church of Santa Maria Maggiore across the piazza. The church has records going further back. At the rectory I learned that the historian only worked from 10:00 a.m. to 12:00 noon. It was now 12:10 p.m. So I was out of luck. Fortunately, the parish priest was there and he gave me a number to call the next day to make an appointment.

Cordenons is a very sleepy town. I could find only one restaurant, and it was closed. Nobody on the streets, no cars, two or three men in every bar. The church bell rang twice at 2:00 p.m. and then twice again at 2:02 p.m.

The next day I called the historian and made an appointment. Two days later, I met with him and found he had already looked up Angelo and traced the DePiero family back to 1606! And not just names of children and parents. Because Italy is a Catholic country and at that time infants did not often survive, they were baptized at birth. So I also received the names of godparents and even the midwife! What a find. These records show that the DePieros were a well-established family in Cordenons when Angelo was born on April 4, 1866.

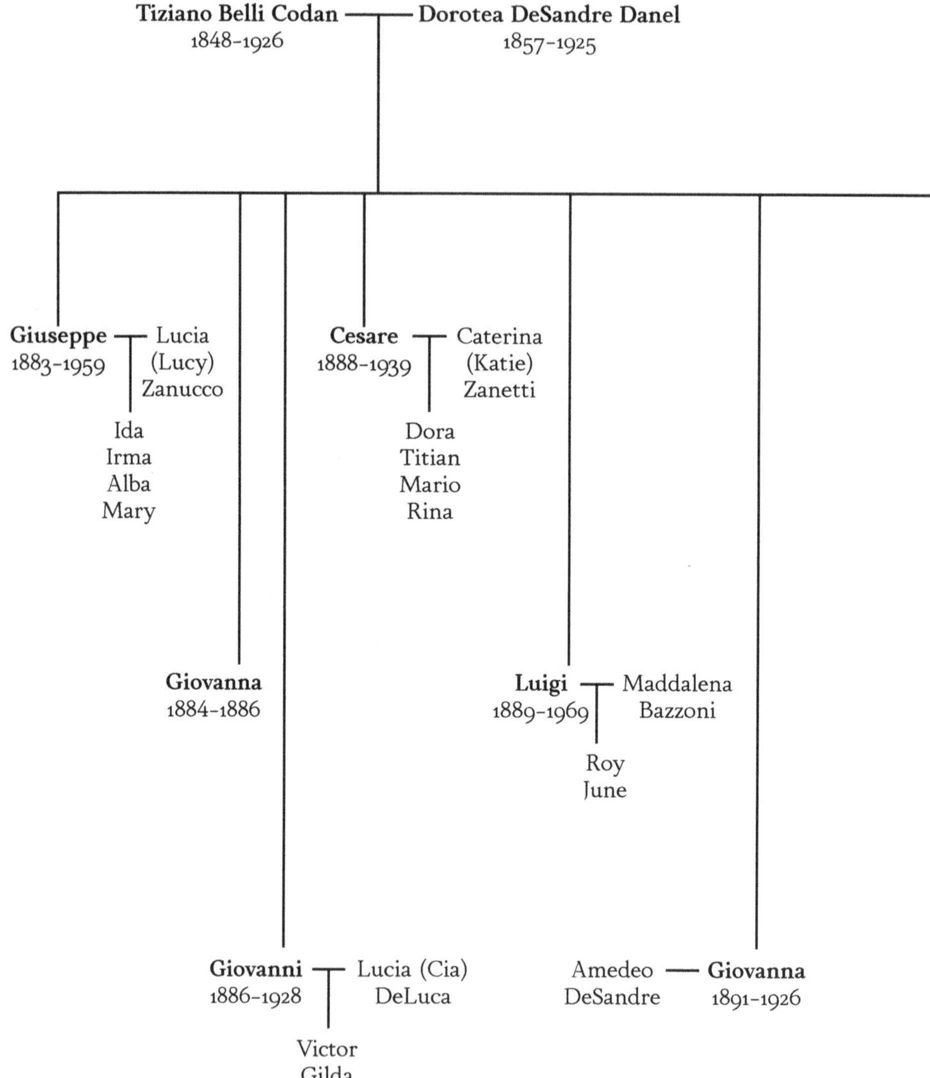

Tiziano Belli Codan
1848-1926
Dorotea DeSandre Danel
1857-1925
Giuseppe
1883-1959
Lucia
(Lucy)
Zanucco
Ida
Irma
Alba
Mary
Cesare
1888-1939
Caterina
(Katie)
Zanetti
Dora
Titian
Mario
Rina
Giovanna
1884-1886
Luigi
1889-1969
Maddalena
Bazzoni
Roy
June
Giovanni
1886-1928
Lucia (Cia)
DeLuca
Victor
Gilda
Amedeo
DeSandre
Giovanna
1891-1926

Belli Family Tree

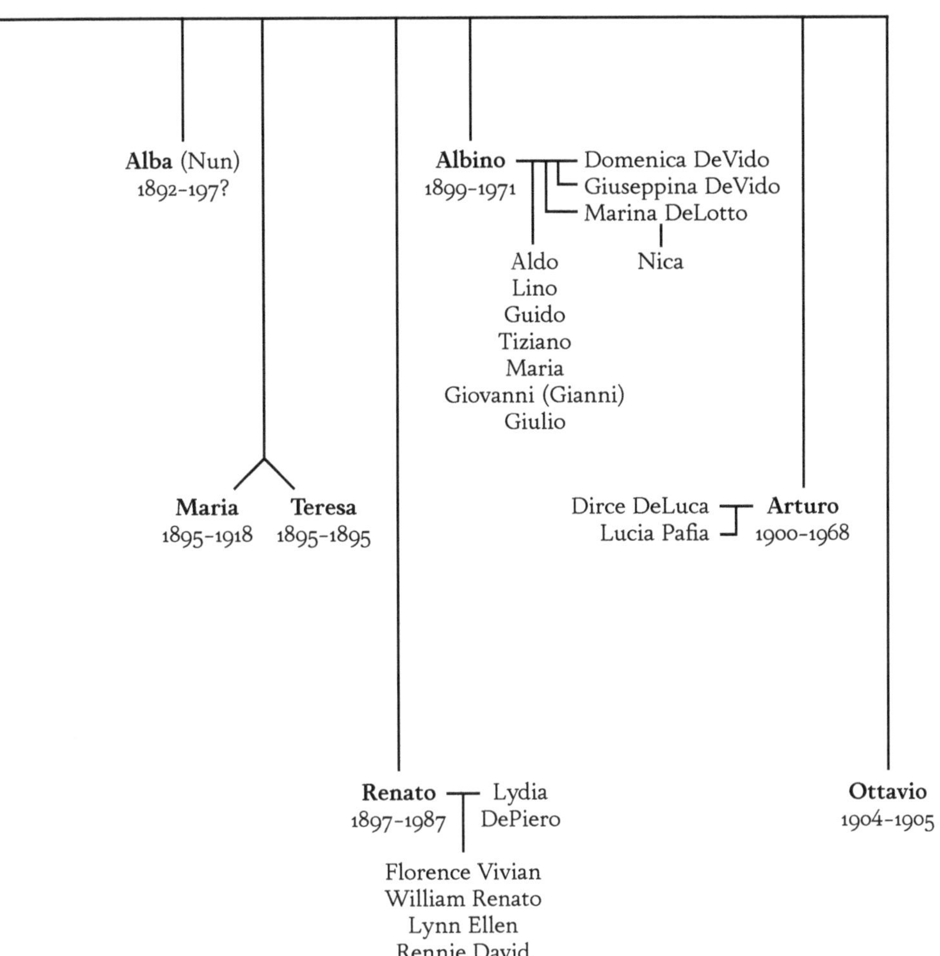

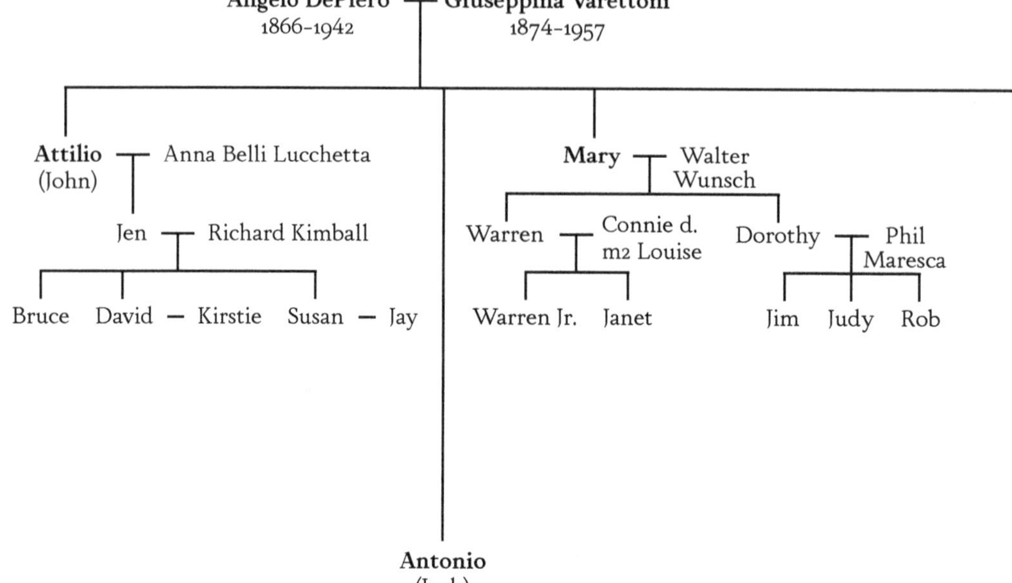
Angelo DePiero
1866-1942
Giuseppina Varettoni
1874-1957
Attilio
(John)
Anna Belli Lucchetta
Jen
Richard Kimball
Bruce
David
Kirstie
Susan
Jay
Antonio
(Jack)
Mary
Walter
Wunsch
Warren
Connie d.
m2 Louise
Dorothy
Phil
Maresca
Warren Jr.
Janet
Jim
Judy
Rob

DePiero Family Tree

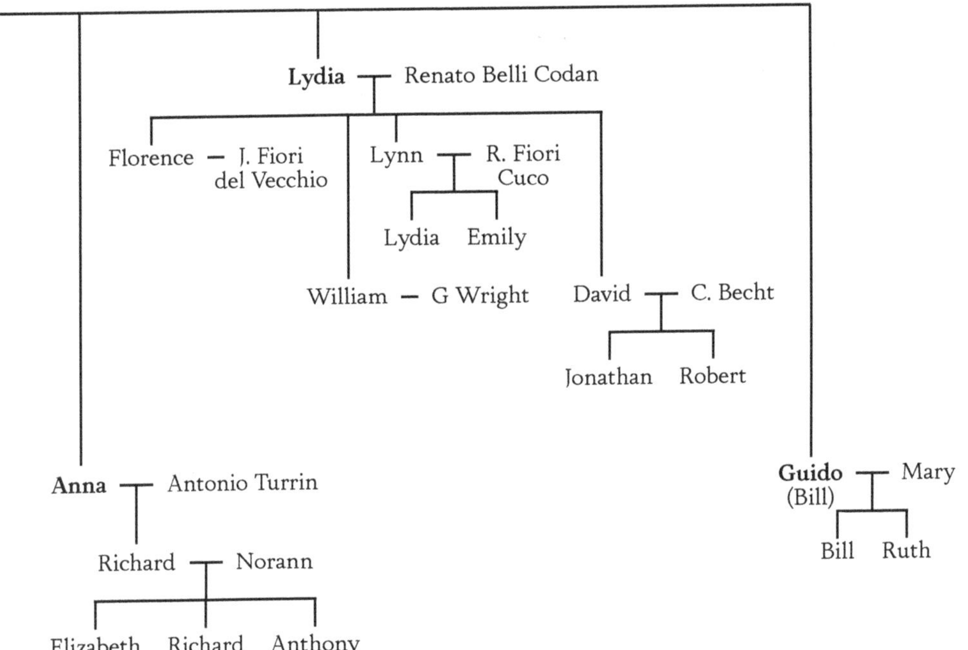

DePiero Family Tree

Giacomo DePiero detto Nut m. Giovanna (Zuanna) deDin daMania
Zuanne (Zanut detto Nut) DePiero 1607–1687 m. Angela della Rossa
Tomaso DePiero b. 1645 m. Luigia Aloisia
Antonio b. 1675 m. Zuanna (Giovanna) Maria Ciprian
Valentino b. 1705 m. Lucia Ongaro
Antonio b. 1736 m. Caterina Venerus
Giacomo b. 1757 m. Agnese Gallin
Luigi b. 1799 m. Angela Zille
Antonio Giuseppe b. 1840 m. Teresa Gardonio del Mul
Angelo Marco 1866–1942 m. Giuseppina Varettoni 1874–1957

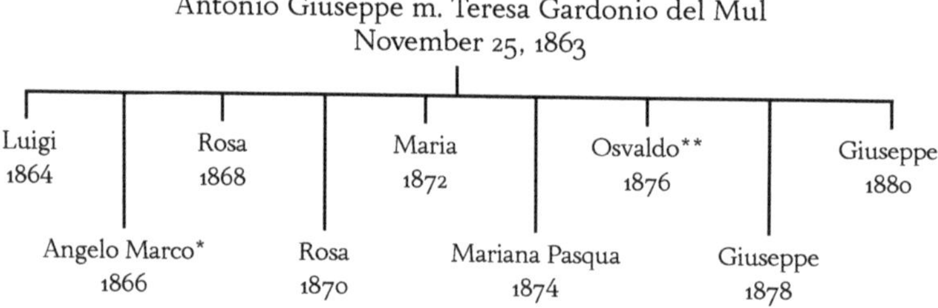

I am assuming Rosa (1868) and Giuseppe (1878) died in infancy. It was common at that time to give the name of a deceased infant to the next child born of the same gender. (See Renato Belli's two sisters named Giovanna,)

* Father of Lydia DePiero.
** Patriarch of the Park Ridge, N.J., DePieros. Father of Dante and grandfather of Ed.

Belli-DePiero Family Tree

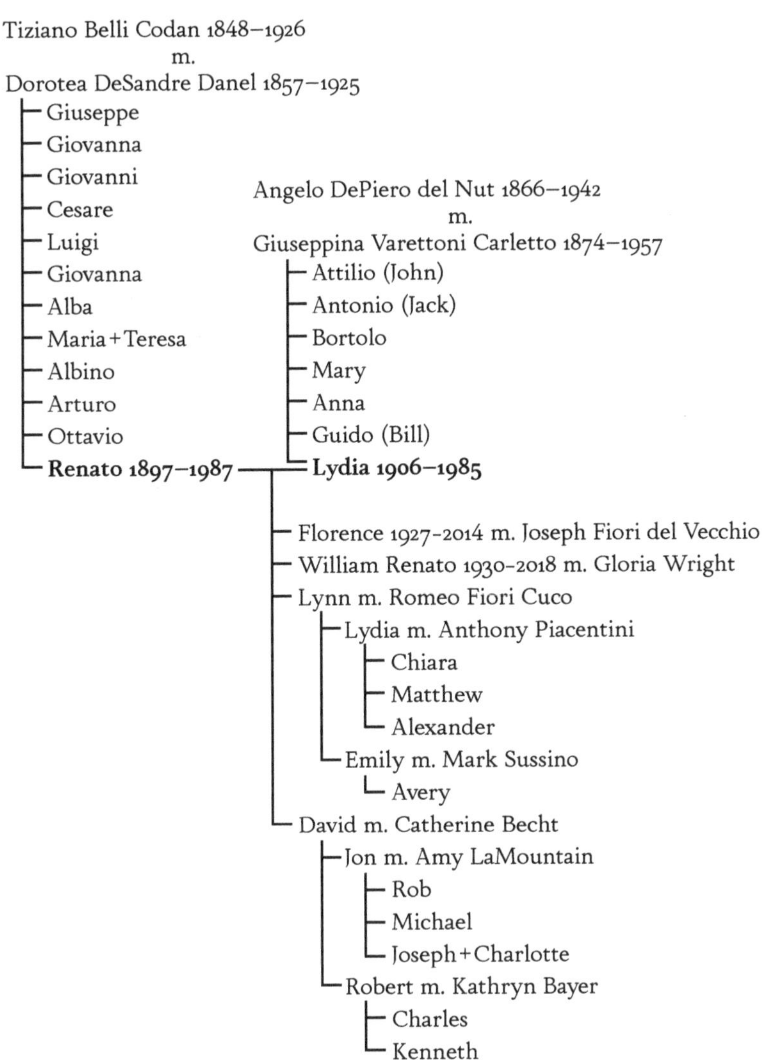

Tiziano Belli Codan 1848–1926
m.
Dorotea DeSandre Danel 1857–1925

- Giuseppe
- Giovanna
- Giovanni
- Cesare
- Luigi
- Giovanna
- Alba
- Maria + Teresa
- Albino
- Arturo
- Ottavio
- **Renato 1897–1987**

Angelo DePiero del Nut 1866–1942
m.
Giuseppina Varettoni Carletto 1874–1957

- Attilio (John)
- Antonio (Jack)
- Bortolo
- Mary
- Anna
- Guido (Bill)
- **Lydia 1906–1985**

Renato 1897–1987 m. **Lydia 1906–1985**

- Florence 1927-2014 m. Joseph Fiori del Vecchio
- William Renato 1930-2018 m. Gloria Wright
- Lynn m. Romeo Fiori Cuco
  - Lydia m. Anthony Piacentini
    - Chiara
    - Matthew
    - Alexander
  - Emily m. Mark Sussino
    - Avery
- David m. Catherine Becht
  - Jon m. Amy LaMountain
    - Rob
    - Michael
    - Joseph + Charlotte
  - Robert m. Kathryn Bayer
    - Charles
    - Kenneth

www.ingramcontent.com/pod-product-compliance
Lightning Source LLC
LaVergne TN
LVHW051937100826
845154LV00001B/5
9781887043960